CREATIVE Awakening

A Guide to *THE ZONE* for Seekers and Makers

by Kristina Coggins

CREATIVE AWAKENING: A GUIDE TO THE ZONE *FOR SEEKERS AND MAKERS*

Published by: New Possible Press in Scottsdale, Arizona

Interior Artwork/Graphics: Kristina Coggins

Cover and Interior Typography: Diane M. Serpa, GreyCatDot Digital Design

Content Editor: Mary L. Holden

Copy Editor: Bill Worth

Library of Congress Cataloging-in-Publication Data is available through the library of congress.

ISBN: 978-0-578-74330-1 (print)

ISBN: 978-0-578-74386-8 (eBook)

This book is dedicated to

Dorothy Cannon,
creative muse and mentor.

With me
in spirit
always.

CONTENTS

FOREWORD

You know how some people are great at talking about being creative: full of theories, and techniques, and lots of opinions? They read books and go to workshops, but they don't actually create very much. Or when they do, it always feels rather precious and heavy.

Thank goodness Kristina Coggins is not one of those people. In fact, you hold in your hands one of the bravest, most alive books on creativity I've ever read. Every page shimmers with her extraordinary natural gift to create freely and generously, while leading others to do the same.

I wish I could play a private movie for you—a movie made of all the images I treasure from my 27 years of friendship with Kristina. Images that pulse with beauty, connection, color, curiosity, and most of all, joy. My movie might start with the first time I walked into her Los Feliz cottage and thought to myself, "What a welcoming space. How did she learn to make a home like this?"

I might show you Kristina holding her newborn son, Sam, on her back porch when she suddenly throws back her head and laughs with the purest happiness. Or maybe I'd show you her ceramics; in particular the small reclining figure of a woman that I've coveted for years because of how it made me feel.

Perhaps I'd include a soundtrack of Kristina's successful acting career, or later, the sounds of her teaching acting to kids. I would have to show you her living room on a day I came to visit after moving away, and staggered backward, overcome by her paintings covering the walls: the colors, the liveliness, the abundance. I'd certainly show you how she kept creating through the kind of heartbreak that would mute most women. Most of all, I'd try to capture how she never questioned her creative urges but tended to them as lovingly as she did her family.

There are a million people telling you how to be creative. What's different about this book is, where others theorize, Kristina lives. She embodies the fullness of expression we all crave. Trust her to help you get out of your own way and let life flow through your hands, your eyes, your heart, and out into the world.

I can't imagine a better guide to the true creative life than Kristina Coggins. There is nothing between you and what you seek. Her wisdom will help you live that.

I am so pleased you'll meet my friend and share her glow.

~ Jennifer Louden

A pioneer of the self-care movement since 1992, Jennifer Louden is the author of The Women's Comfort Book, The Women's Retreat Book, The Life Organizer, and, Why Bother: Discover the Desire for What's Next. *She has spoken around the U.S., Canada, and Europe, and has written a national magazine column for a Martha Stewart magazine. She's been profiled or quoted in dozens of major magazines, and pieces of her wisdom appear in two of Brené Brown's books (*Daring Greatly *and* Dare to Lead*). Jennifer has appeared on hundreds of TV shows (including "Oprah"), radio programs, and podcasts. Her website is www.jenniferlouden.com.*

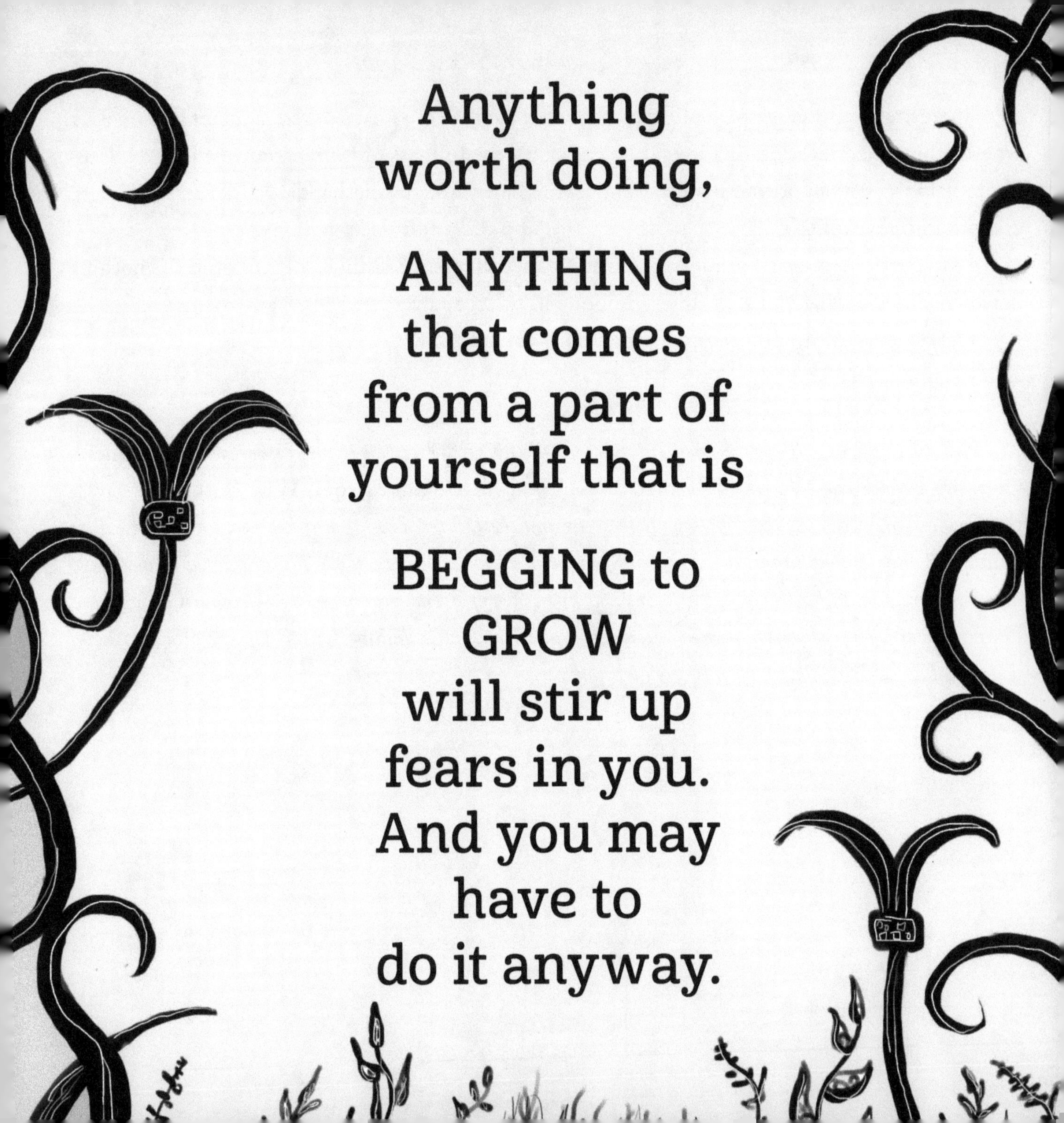

Anything
worth doing,

ANYTHING
that comes
from a part of
yourself that is

BEGGING to
GROW
will stir up
fears in you.
And you may
have to
do it anyway.

INTRODUCTION

In all my years on this planet, the happiest and most fulfilled I have ever been is when I'm expressing myself—being a creative. I have worked and played as an actress, painter, storyteller, director, poet, writer, and a creative life coach. I've played in the dirt, made pottery, designed clothing and costumes, painted theatre sets, decoupaged cigar boxes, created greeting cards, and tried to sing country western songs like Patsy Cline (which brought hilarity to my family). I have had the luxury of being creative my whole life.

I also use creativity to guide my clients to discover their own expressions and find deep fulfillment in the process.

In my years as a life and creativity coach, the single most positive change I have watched in people, even the so called "non-creatives," is when they start to make stuff again—to create something out of nothing but a seed of an idea. As a result, they walk with more confidence, they are more curious about the world and they have more energy. Their eyes are bright and alive, and their faces soften. They find a connection to their spiritual energy that is sustaining and generative. Their relationships improve. They are kinder and gentler. They are more playful and spontaneous.

How is it that connecting to one's own creative force can affect this kind of change?

We are all makers and have been since the beginning of opposable thumbs.

Creativity is a basic, human, God-granted, cellular imperative, and a right.

For years, we've lived in a culture that implied the only identity worth pursuing is the one that produces financial rewards. Creativity is for hobbyists—unless you were born with artistic genius like Michelangelo or van Gogh. When you buy this belief, you are robbed of your drive to express this natural force and create with honor.

Humanity is entering a new age—an age where technology is no longer the new art form. This new age will keep you searching for meaning and ideas through concept. Developing and using a creative, innovative mindset and operating system is the direction people and businesses are going. For companies seeking innovation, creative thinkers are the new sages. For people like you who seek more joy in life, creativity is the new currency.

My intention is to free you to pick up the longings and the tools that you've been turning your back on. My intention is to inspire you to rebel from past societal strictures and do that *one thing* that's been in the back of your mind or lodged within your heart. My intention is to give you tools to get into the zone and to learn to get in this state consciously, and to express what's inside you in new ways. My intention is to have you experience the power of your own creativity and to use the power of the zone, or flow, in your own life. The experience of expressing your creativity in the zone is like a gateway drug for empowerment and wholeness. It helps you live a longer, happier life and gives you a sense of purpose. It also provides an avenue for a deep connection to a spiritual source.

You were attracted to this book because you knew something was looking to find you. You might be trying to answer a call that is coming deep inside of you, or you may have had some curiosity about something that has been begging for you to express. Something in you must know that those people who actively create from their own hearts and impulses are amongst the happiest and most fulfilled people in the world.

To break down and explain creativity's mysteries for you, I've borrowed information from expert sources on topics as broad as: neuroscience, meditation, spirituality, mindfulness, and positive psychology. I've included the wisdom of my own experiences, in addition to those of my clients.

It is my hope that you will find inspiration, support, and encouragement to claim your God-given right to be a maker and experience the profound rewards that creative expression has for you. Wherever that will lead you is always part of the mystery.

Follow the
TRAIL
of your
LONGINGS

PART ONE: THE CLEARING

Like sediment that drops to the bottom of the glass before it can be unclouded, the blockages you carry with you must also be cleared. To reach creative clarity, your past wounds, misconceptions, and past beliefs, can be dropped so your purest parts (the original creative impulse) can be revealed.

The *One Thing*

There is this thing that has been in your heart or mind, and it won't leave you alone. It's your desire to paint, to work with wood, to design clothes, or, perhaps to write. You may have had this desire and curiosity for a very long time, or it may have been slowly growing over time, until one day it comes to the forefront and makes demands: "DRAW ME! DANCE ME! SING ME! MAKE ME! PLEASE."

Imagine being asked by someone you trusted, "What is the *one thing* you still want to do?"

If you were honest with them and yourself, you'd start by saying, "I've always wanted…

…to sell things I craft or knit.

…to write a book.

…to make sculptures.

…to carve marble.

…to sing.

…to paint.

…to make prints.

…to design and sew clothing.

…to dance.

…to make bread.

…to make furniture.

…to garden.

…to tell stories.

…to design video games.

…to narrate audio books.

…to write poetry.

…to photograph buildings.

…to create a podcast.

…to play an instrument.

…to become a clown.

The possibilities are endless, and diverse. If you have a song to sing or some making to do, the desire to do it will come from deep within. Maybe you picked up this book to get some inspiration or to find courage to bring it into fruition. You may suspect that finding the courage to act on your creative desire will change you. You haven't created yet because you don't have support from your outside world to do this thing. You have no time to create. Perhaps you think, "It's just too crazy." There are a million reasons—and you have one or two. This longing, however, remains with you. It will stick with you. It's both patient and kind. It's waiting.

If this feels familiar, you are not alone. Everyone has their own *one thing* inside them—the *one thing* they want to create before they die. This *one thing*, when you really allow yourself to think of it, feels like joy and curiosity. Where did it come from? Could it be that a force beyond yourself has been calling your name? Can you feel it waiting for you?

This book is designed to inspire you to do your *one thing*.

The No-Regret Zone

Regret. Comedian Lucille Ball said, "I'd rather regret the things I've done than regret the things I haven't done." On their dying day, people regret things like having worked too much and not followed their calling or curiosity. Or, they'll regret not having listened to themselves and their hearts, instead of listening to and performing according to the expectations of others.

Creative expression leads the way to a life of no regrets. By its very nature, creativity requires your inner rebel to be at play, to dash some societal expectations, and forge ahead on your own. The simple act of following your creative call will lead to fresh playgrounds where no regrets can grow. Following the nagging nudge of your *one thing* is a courageous act which will serve the whole of your life.

For every decision I have needed to make, I have asked an old woman for advice. Who is she? She is my vision of me, at the end of my life. I usually ask her, "Would you be proud of me if I…?"

She is a great source of wisdom. Her answers may confirm my inner knowing, or, she surprises me. She has answers ready with a chuckle, a twinkle in her eye, or a smart-ass remark, but she always has generous regard for my struggle, and an unconditional appreciation for my spirit. She assists me in living in the No-Regret Zone.

What would your elder person say to you about doing the *one thing* that keeps calling you? Would he/she be disappointed in you at the end of your life it you didn't do it?

When you feel regret, it is usually accompanied by shame or guilt. Those two emotions are some of the most unfortunate and uncomfortable feelings to have floating around your body. Here's an empowering question to ask your current self: "What shall I do today to live, love, and die without regret?

I believe that people's dreams never die. Your dream of expressing yourself in creative ways will either come true—or you'll take it to your grave. It's your choice. This idea may create anxiety for you.

I have come to believe that the anxiety I feel when I'm not writing, painting, or standing up for my dream is a gift. I tell myself the anxious feeling I get when I don't follow through is the best of me. It's the old woman in me who is providing messages through my body. It's her way of showing me the way into the No-Regret Zone.

What shall I
do today to
live, love,
and die
without regret?

Have a Healthy Revolt

We have all been duped by a culture that says it's all about how we work, what we produce for the market, how we provide for ourselves and loved ones, and, what we look like or own. Our culture wants to make worker bees out of us. This plan is to the detriment of our happiness and fulfillment. It's like being in a kind of jail.

Are you tired of your jail time with this culture? If you are, a healthy revolt feels good. You can claim your real life and take no prisoners.

You, like many people, are overworked and feel stress. Perhaps you think that struggle and hard work is an indication of your worthiness in society and to your family. You give until it hurts. But this kind of pain is not a virtue. You are burdened. You are out of harmony with the rhythm of your own nature.

When you connect to a feeling of righteous indignation, you'll likely find radical and healthy retribution. The cost of suppressing your creativity is profound—personally, and culturally. Will you wait until it's considered socially appropriate (in retirement) to produce watercolor paintings? You could wait until your kids are in college to write your memoir. Waiting puts a lot of happy on the back burner in order to follow the rules.

Use the healthy energy of anger to take back your life. Use that energy for good. What is the *one thing* that is trying to find you? Find the *one thing* that lights you up and turn it into action by reclaiming your impulses to create. How have you turned away from your creative impulse because it wasn't deemed worthwhile by your family or culture? There are creative waters in every human being. You can tap into yours by using curiosity, desire, and willingness to show up. Forget the idea that you need to have been born with a talent. Have a desire. Show up and begin.

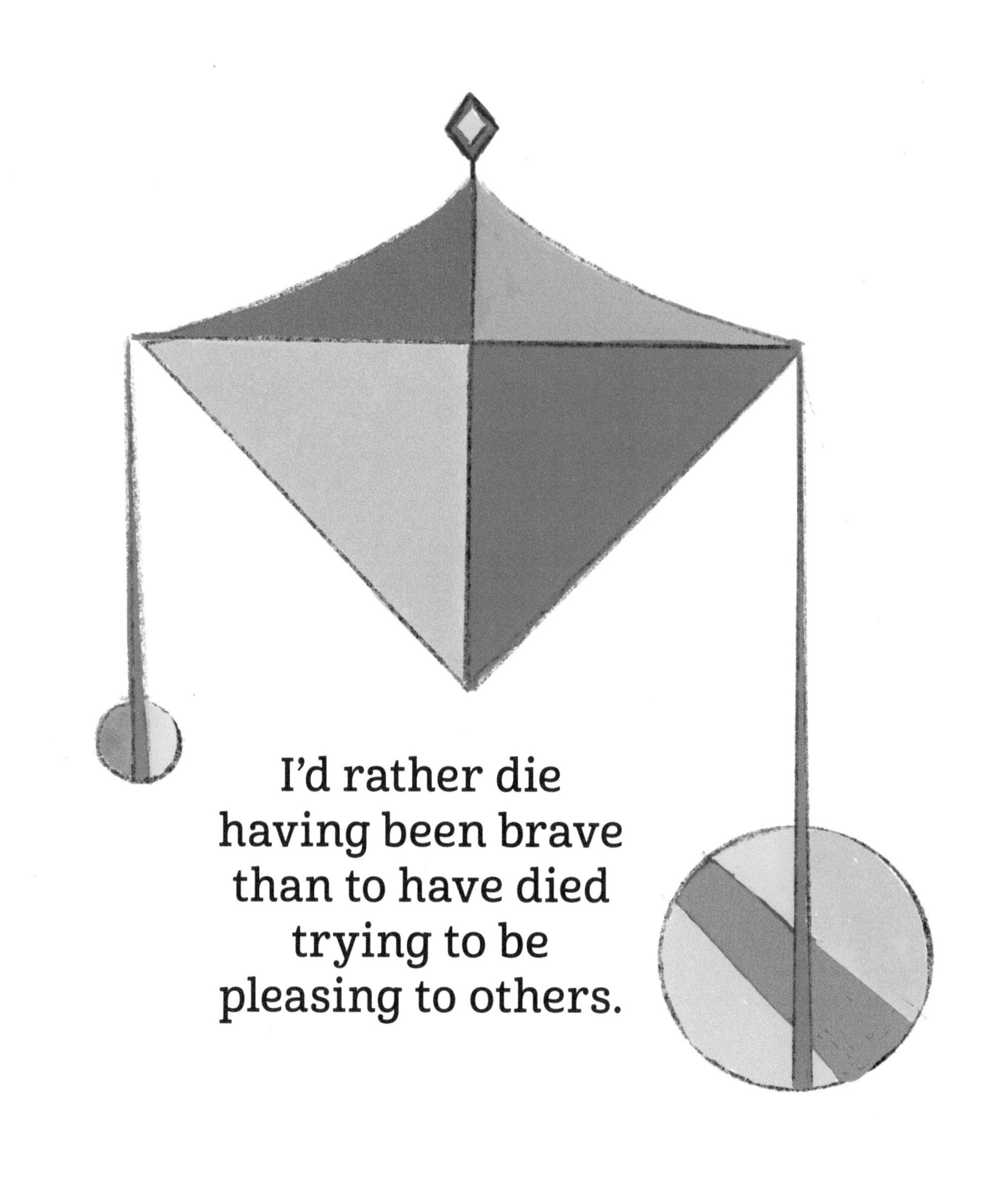
I'd rather die
having been brave
than to have died
trying to be
pleasing to others.

If Not You, Then Who?

What if you were picked for doing this *one thing*? There must be a reason you have this longing and curiosity to write songs, direct theatre, carve wood, or write a book. There must be a reason you suddenly get a line stuck in your head that will not go away until you realize it's a poem and you must sit down and write the damn thing. What if you have no time for this nonsense, but you can't help wanting to do it?

Is it possible that there is an energy coming from your source that keeps giving you the inexplicable drive to make the thing? Is it possible that you were chosen to do your *one thing* based on unique qualities you have? Why were you picked? Why are you uniquely suited to paint this painting, sing a song, or write that book or poem? Was it something in your history, a longing to get some feeling out of your cells and out to the world? Why are you uniquely qualified? Was it your background? Is there some aspect of your own life story that people would benefit by knowing? Why were you cast as someone who could play the role required to do your *one thing*? What is in your essence that will touch other people?

Ask yourself, "If not me, then who?" Let your senior self answer, and, if you still don't know, let it be a mystery. But, also know that you must begin to create. Believe that this longing you have to do your *one thing* is never random. It is always there for a reason.

Making Amends to Yourself

If you, like most people, feel a calling that you've been too afraid to materialize, then join the Human Club. The *one thing* you have desired to do has been put off, due to all kinds of excuses. Don't beat yourself up. It's not hopeless. Hang in there with me.

Maybe it wasn't time to bring your *one thing* into form. Art has its own time schedule. If this notion resonates with you, good!

It's more likely however, that you've suppressed the desire to create your *one thing* because you had other values that were in competition. Busy parents may long for time alone to paint. Perhaps you have a demanding job but you long to take piano lessons so you can write these songs you have inside you. Values are often in competition, but for some reason, this one desire is now finally sliding to the forefront. Something in your life has shifted, your curiosity is getting ramped up. You feel the time is now—your need to create is the value that is winning the competition.

You need forgiveness to clear the way. When you recognize the pain that being squelched has caused you, and can forgive yourself, you honor yourself in a way that is filled with compassion. You start to own your desires. Oh, it's so easy to say you start to love yourself because that sounds so horrendously trite. But it's true. Tenderness for self is a powerful shift.

Apologize to those parts of you that have been squelched because you thought it was the right thing to do. Tell them, "I'm going to honor you now. I'm going to listen." You will feel them relax as they sense you have their back. Say, "I'm listening now. Let's work together." Here are some healing words for all who have been silenced:

> *I'm sorry. I'm sorry your light was dimmed, your voice was silenced, and your senses were numbed. I'm sorry your truth was squelched. I'm sorry your curiosity, excitement, and love*

were dialed down so that you'd feel belonging and acceptance from others. I'm sorry your sense of obligation to work or family caused you to decide not to pursue your desire to express your creativity. I feel your original spirit. It is now time to return to your innocence where you can use your curiosity, time, and attention to express yourself with your making. There are people waiting for you to show up.

What Will You Grow?

Being a parent will challenge you, change you, and grow you. The responsibility of parenting allows you to find a deeper love than you could ever imagine possible.

Being a performance athlete will test your fortitude, grow your confidence, and develop a strong lean body and six-pack abs.

Becoming an artist and an expressor of your creativity will also change you. If you make a practice of being in *the zone* (or flow), you will be even more profoundly changed. If you commit to a practice of making, here are just some of the benefits you can expect from experiencing the flow on a regular basis.

- Courage
- An ability to ask for support from others
- Self-worth
- Cultivation of the art of distraction free living
- The practice of something which will lead to mastery
- Connecting to mysterious and magical forces
- Awareness of synchronicities
- Trust in self
- A connection to source
- Honoring self
- Being honest and authentic with self and others
- Self-confidence
- Tenderness for self and others
- The skills to defer self-gratification
- Mental toughness
- The capacity to endure adversity, injustice, indifference, criticism
- Humility
- Increased ability to focus
- Lack of self-consciousness
- The ability to receive and appreciate constructive criticism
- Stillness
- Oneness
- Awareness of your mind's chatter and an ability to quiet it

- An increased sensitivity to the sensations in your body
- The ability to inquire and challenge your previously held beliefs that no longer serve
- Inner radiance
- Increased energy
- Better awareness and appreciation for your intuition
- Development of new skill sets
- A love of learning
- A connection to the source of it all
- A relationship with forces beyond yourself
- A feeling of support from forces beyond you
- A better relationship to loneliness and existential dread
- A sense of personal power
- The ability to be comfortable in your own skin
- A sense of peace
- A sense of joy in simplicity
- Development of your own style
- Better ability to use your voice and advocate for self
- An increased energetic vibration
- A sense of aliveness
- Connection with a tribe of individuals who share your passions
- Support from like-minded people
- Contribution to the world
- Becoming a master of your craft as well as yourself

But What Do You Really Want?

What do you really want? What is this curiosity about? Once it shows up, you must decide about what to do with it. What's it worth to you? Well-being? To feel that your soul's calling is being answered? An opportunity to connect with others who share a common interest? A feeling of alignment with source?

Be honest with yourself about what you want. It could be a passing curiosity that you explore that leads you to something else. It could be knitting that will help you learn to be still. It could be that coloring could restore your nervous system after trauma. It could be that you want to experience self-growth through writing. You could sense that by painting you would experience a connection to your higher power/source. You may want to be more innovative at work and push outside the constraints of the current systems of operation. You may want to finish a book that you have inside of you; to speak, and teach. You may want to write a blog and build a community of people who'll support you. You may want to join a class of printers so that you have a community of artists.

All are worthy pursuits, and all are possible with creative expression.

Ask yourself: What are my reasons for wanting to pursue this curiosity? What might I experience that would enhance my life? What are the costs of not pursuing this?

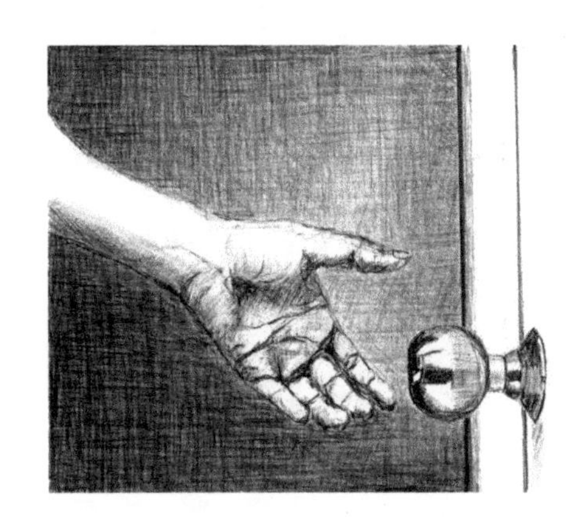

Our brains
crave the new.

Where is the sweet
spot between
what we know
and
what we
yearn
to express
for the first time?

Values and Time

Think of all that is on your list of things to be done. Like everyone else, you need to make money to put food on the table, to eat the food, to rest and digest the food, then to exercise to keep the food from turning into fat. It takes time and energy and money to be a "list ninja."

The things you do that are truly fulfilling do not always bring in money. For example: loving, connecting, traveling, playing, resting, and making art. To live a fulfilling life, you need to make space for the *one thing* that fills you up. When you take the time to fill yourself up, you have more energy and engagement for things on the regular to-do list. You must make time for the *one thing* that fills up your soul.

I believe in taking a sober and honest look at making reasonable time for creating. If you don't, the lack of creative time turns into yet another exercise in guilt and shame. If your priorities are work and family, to expect to write a book in a month is nearly impossible (unless you get your people to support you during National Novel Writing Month in November). When November is too far away, you might be able to devote time and energy to write for 45 minutes in the morning before everyone wakes up or after your kids are in bed for the night.

Once you get clear about your conflicting values of being a good family member and a writer, the only thing you can control is the energy and time you can give to both. This is a choice. It includes not choosing to be a victim, but an advocate for yourself.

Question the beliefs you unconsciously are holding about your creative self by filling in the blanks:

I want ____,

but can't have/do it, because ________________________________.

The truth is, even if at this point in your life you only have time for 30 minutes a day of writing, just knowing you have a choice will improve your life satisfaction level enough to make a difference. Many books have been written in 30-minute segments of time that have been carved out of a lunch break, or, sacrificed from TV watching or sleeping.

I give you permission to question the beliefs that are holding you back. My intention is to provide you with the support you can create, both internally and externally, in order to bring your desires to the forefront and finally act on them.

What is the Source?

At the end of the book by Frances Hodgson Burnett, *The Secret Garden*, there is a quote I love. "Do you believe in magic?" Colin asks Mrs. Sowerby when she first sees the blooming garden that has been transformed by the children. She tells him that yes, she does believe in magic and it doesn't matter what you call it, it's all a part of the "big good thing." The "big good thing" doesn't worry, it goes on making worlds by the million. It's the joy that matters, and she reminds him that he was singing to it when she entered the garden.

What is the "big good thing?" It is the relationship you will have with forces outside yourself when creating in *the zone* and using the force of your own creativity.

Some people use the Greek idea of "the Muses" for the kind of energy that provides nudges, ideas, and inspiration. But this energy has always been a mystery. Others use the concepts of the higher self, angels, guides, the universe, universal spirit, the divine, the creator, the Source, or God. For people who trust science, this energy might be known as the quantum field, the field of infinite possibility, or the universal intelligence. Whatever you believe from a spiritual or scientific perspective, doesn't matter. When dealing with human creativity, it does not matter what you call its source. What matters in creativity is that when you free your mind from chatter, get still, and begin to enter the forcefield that is *the zone*, you will receive guidance and inspiration.

Some artists explain it by saying," I just got out of the way. It came through me." Well, where in the love of heaven did it come from? When people say this, it is usually because they sense that their work is being supplied or delivered—and perhaps supported—by someone or something else.

It's simple. Creativity is both of you and beyond you. The more you practice this state of being and your relationship to the "big good thing," the more fulfilling your creative life will be. You will thrive. Words and dogma do not matter to the experience of creating. Creativity's source is neither from your ego or your mind. It is from your heart.

Your Life Force

Put your energy into expressing your life force. When it comes to reclaiming your creativity, there are techniques, philosophies, processes, and strategies for uncovering all your broken places that keep you from expressing your creativity. There are webinars and groups designed to help unstick you from negative forces. You can exert all your energy into "therapizing" and “therapuking” the reason you are not doing the calling of your soul. You can blame yourself and call yourself a saboteur till the cows come home. All you will be left with is shame and guilt.

It’s simpler than that. Every person has a life force that wants to be expressed. Humans are the only mammals on planet Earth that impede the natural flow of life’s force by using their big, important brains. If we think of our creativity as our life force, as a natural thing—like an animal, a tree, or a river—we would spend less time analyzing and more time making things with our heads, hearts, and hands.

Do one simple thing today that expresses your life force. It could be making something in your yard beautiful, whittling a stick, rearranging your drawer to make finding things easy and attractive, making a salad using berries from the bush outside. Notice how the flow of that force makes you feel better. More relaxed, more centered, more yourself. It doesn’t matter whether you’re carving marble for a museum exhibit, or decorating a room for your daughter, it’s all the same.

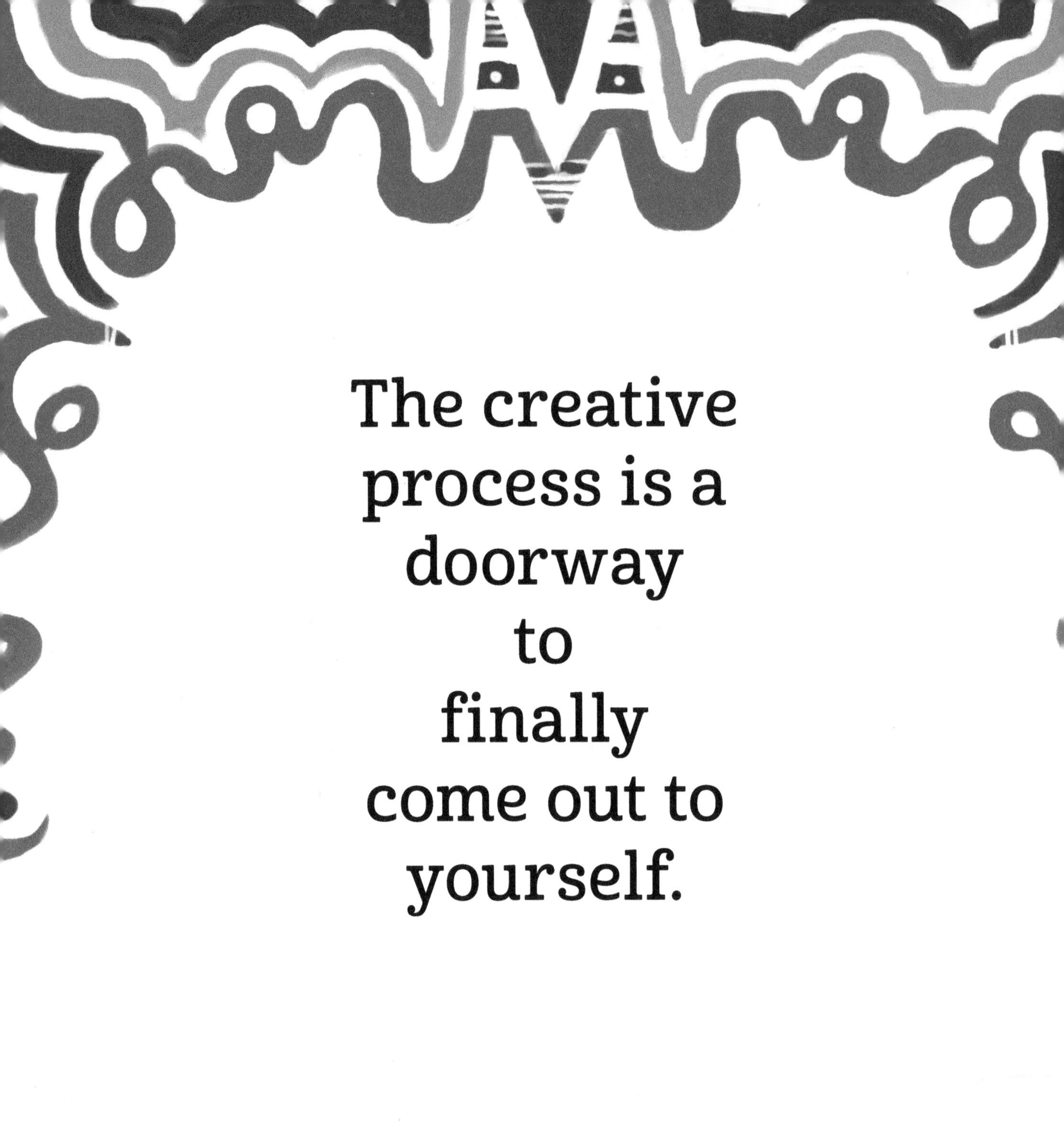

The creative
process is a
doorway
to
finally
come out to
yourself.

It's Just Making

Many years ago, I was working at a job in training and development. At the time, I thought it was the only way for me to make money. "Art is for hobbying," I thought. I wasn't somebody who could claim those artistic impulses in myself at the time. My longings could never be counted on to make money.

Else Tamayo, a gifted artist and fellow co-worker saw something in me. Perhaps it was that I didn't fit in to this work culture or my penchant for "artsy things," I don't know, but she took me under her wing. She must have seen an unrecognized, hidden artist in me and through her eyes, I saw myself differently. She was slightly older, and we shared an interest in art and painting. She did it though; I only talked about it at that time.

On my birthday, she handmade a mobile for me with a quote by Corita Kent: "We have no art. We do everything as well as we can. The only way is 'make.' There are no rules for leaping into the unknown, because nobody has ever been there before."

This saying stayed with me. It has guided me and reminded me. Creativity is a verb, not a thing, not an identity. You and I learn to become creative beings by doing and being. I share this with you because for me, it is the cornerstone for freeing myself to express my work.

Romantic Notions Dashed

Do you have romantic notions of what artists do all day? Perhaps a beautiful painter who has dappled light coming into her studio, she's wearing gauze, and opera music plays in the background. Maybe a guitarist who is suddenly moved to create his masterpiece one afternoon and doesn't come up for air until the last chord is written.

The truth is, most art is like life: A series of challenges brought on by the artist's own resistance or creative blocks. Some of these challenges look like lack of time, misunderstandings in relationships, worries about lack, fears about artistic integrity, the dread of a dream not coming to fruition. Do you think you cannot be an artist if you are also a responsible adult?

When I was an actress, I was told by mentors that if I didn't have to be an actress, then, for God's sake, do something else. Why this advice? The chances of success are slim. The business is difficult. So, if you don't have to be creative, don't. If you do, it will only force you to grow beyond yourself to see what you are made of. Do you need that trouble? (Yes, you do.)

You want to have access to the deeper truth of yourself. You want to create a life of meaning and have no regrets. Welcome to the tribe. Be prepared for a deeper spiritual connection and true fulfillment.

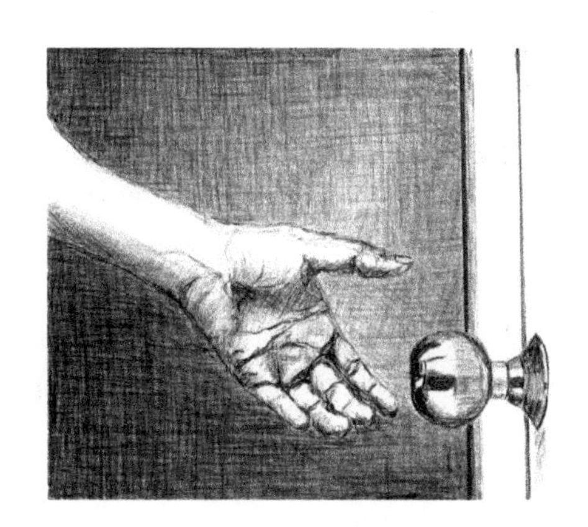

The Wizard

I was teaching a group of children in an after-school acting class. They were in the age range of 7-10. A few of their faces showed skepticism, but some were eager. I had no idea how to get them inspired and felt as if I didn't know what I was doing as I spoke to them about the concept of having an inner wizard. Their faces lit up, and I continued. I said their wizard grows when it is honored and heard. The inner wizard must be treated well so it so could grow bigger and have a louder voice.

Later, I taught a group of teenagers, and hesitantly brought up the same concept, only trying to be hipper and more conversational. Their faces lit up, too!

When I took the inner wizard concept to a class for adults…same!

What was the reason that concept resonated with all age groups? I believe it was the truth that your inner wizard is an entity (made of genius energy) that wants to get your attention and encourage you to do the *one thing* you need to do. Your wizard is waving his wand around inside of you, empowering you to use your magical gifts. That's what all the hubbub of curiosity and longing and anxiety has been about!

Honor your wizard. It is the part of you that is genius. You may not have tapped into it yet, but trust me, you do have it. You're in the position of having an inspiration, you have a project, a creation, and you want to put your work into the world. You want to see it. You want others to see it. The genius will help you when you get out of your own way. Take a breath and let it help you with a strategy, with technology problems, inspiration delays, means of financial support.

Here's an important hint: The genius doesn't seem to believe in time like you do. It goes slowly, is in no hurry, takes things one step at a time. Your inner wizard sees the whole situation when you get out of the way. It doesn't give a @%**&! if you feel it's too much work! It only cares about channeling itself and using you as a vehicle.

There was a reason you were given curiosity about what you might create. There was a reason your gifts are calling. They want to be born! They want you to use them.

Artists Are Happy

Why do artists who are actively making their art look more alive than other people? Why, after a couple of hours of making their art, are their faces softer? Why do they move with more fluidity? Their eyes seem brighter and their smiles come more easily when they've given themselves over to their creative natures. What is it about art that makes artists feel more alive, refreshed, and new? Is it because after they've been making, they feel satisfied? Maybe they've had a little "spirit dusting?"

There is a common cultural belief that artists are more depressed and unhappy than the rest of the people in the world. Not true! The research suggests that in fact artists are happier and more psychologically stable than those who are not expressing themselves in some form of creating. Most notable was a massive survey done in 2013 conducted by researchers at the University of Zurich which surveyed happiness levels in various occupations. The results of this study, showing that artists are generally happier than the rest of the population, was published in a 2014 blog in *Psychology Today*, titled, "Happy Artists."

My belief is that we all have an innate need to express ourselves and make art, whether it be in cooking, gardening, or writing the great American novel. And making art can lead you to greater happiness.

From my own experience, and as a witness of my clients, the artists who stop working on their projects are the ones who are depressed and unhappy. Once they return, their energy comes back too, and they feel fulfilled. Even if they begin in small incremental steps, when the blocks to expressing themselves are removed, they gain happiness once more.

Think about the artists/makers you know who are not actively doing their craft. As they are suppressing and denying their expression, you will see constriction in their movements and a duller/flatter expression in their eyes. You will probably hear them give elaborate excuses for why they are not working now. It may involve blaming outside circumstances and others. You may notice whiny, bitter tones in their voices.

But, when you've seen them in the states of discovery, inspiration, or active creation, you've noticed their energy was higher, they were more curious, and they may have even felt a sense of fulfillment. They were less rigid physically—and emotionally. If they had learned to face their discomfort by moving out of their comfort zone, it would stand to reason they'd have begun to say yes to new opportunities and challenges.

Creatives, such as these friends you're thinking of, are more spontaneous; perhaps they've even said things like: "Yes! Let's go. It sounds fun." Artists know that exploration is the key to expansion, because they're able to do it in their studios or offices. Artists who are actively engaged in their making seem to laugh more and take life a little more lightly.

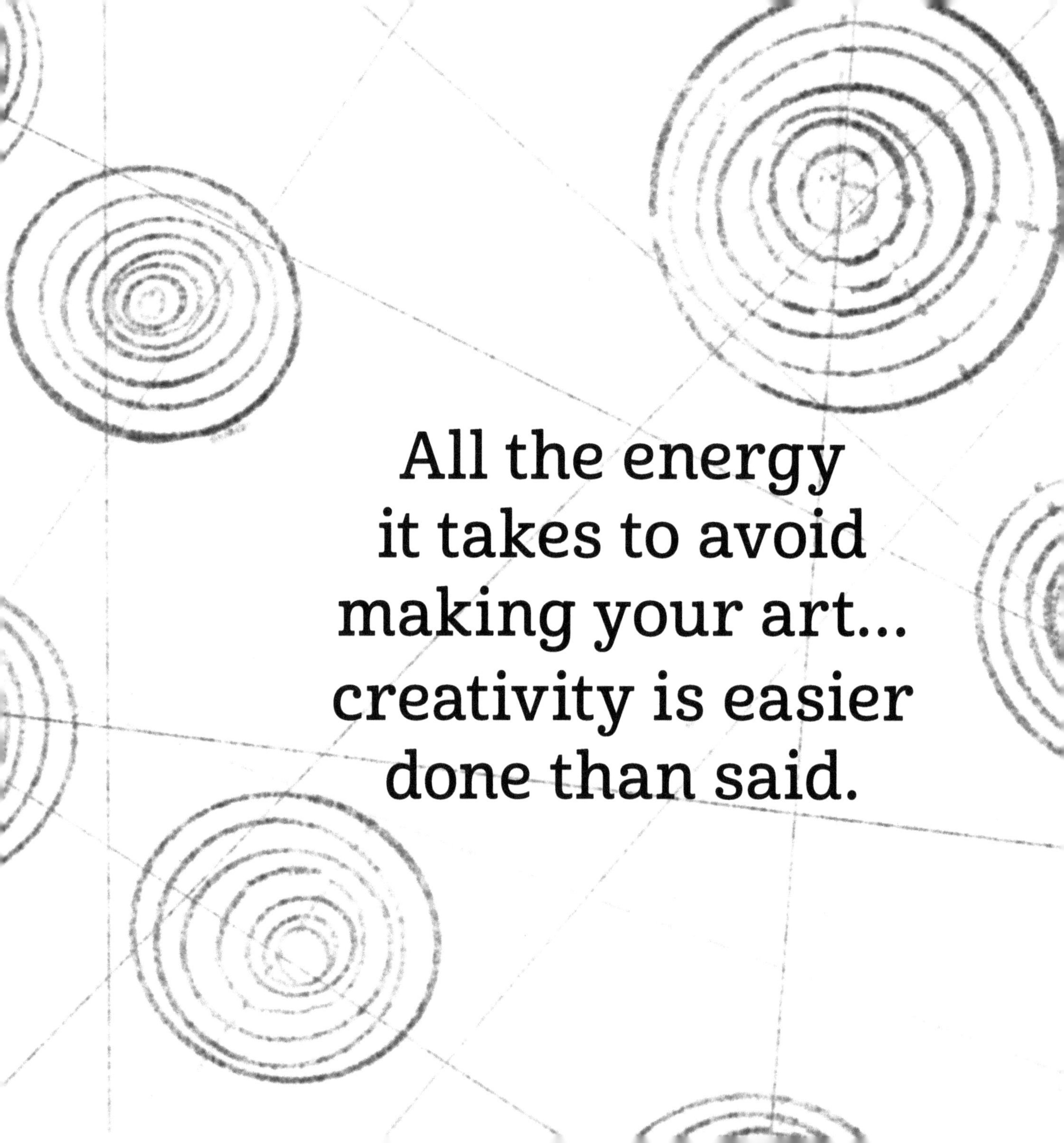
All the energy
it takes to avoid
making your art...
creativity is easier
done than said.

All That Wasted Energy

Think now of the indescribable waste of energy it requires to avoid making your art! The time and energy it takes to distract yourself from that calling that says, "Oh, this could be fun. I could play here. I could grow myself here. I could brighten someone's day with my voice."

Everyone at times gives into the distraction of scrolling through Instagram, binge-watching Netflix, going out with people who are not brave enough to make their art either, or working longer hours in jobs that feed the body but not the soul. It's common to tell yourself that your obligations hold you back; that your spouse or partner won't understand, your children need you, the house needs to be perfect, you don't have enough money to build the perfect artist's studio.

It's all subterfuge.

All these excuses are disguised as "good sense." Right?

No.

You could save so much energy if you'd just do the *one thing* that scares you because it will ultimately lead to happiness and satisfaction. If you think of it, wouldn't all that energy be better used by just starting on your *one thing*? When you do your art for even 15 minutes, you feel better. When you commit to making your art for an hour, you feel amazing. When you make a stand for yourself and make art every day, you change your life—for the better. When you put your art out there in the world, you change other people's lives. You don't know it yet, but there are people waiting for you to show up.

Healing Through Creativity

Expression of your creative desires is a gateway to healing grief. Your creativity enables healing of past wounds and trauma held in your nervous system. After all, you are taking tools and doing something with your body that expresses something inside of yourself.

Writing poems healed me. After my divorce, I wrote poems that expressed raw emotional pain as well as something deeper in me that I was trying to make sense of in this time in my life. This set of poems illuminated deeper truths about my life—truths that were trying to get into my conscious attention. I know I moved through my grief easier because the poetry showed me how. I became accustomed to the ways a poem would nag at me to write it during that time. The experience taught me that when I get a flash of an image or hear some language that surprises me, I know it is a poem asking to be written. I rush to the page and know it will harangue me until I get it out.

After her husband died, Florence started coloring. She bought adult coloring books and colored pens and sat for hours filling in the pictures. She never thought of herself as creative, but she told me that sitting and doing nothing but putting colors on a page was what healed her body and soul after her husband's long illness. She was bemused and embarrassed when she told me about it, but for six months she could do nothing but live inside those colors and designs.

The repetitive movement this kind of coloring requires creates oxytocin, known as the "feel good hormone." Both oxytocin and the stillness quieted Florence's nervous system after the trauma. She showed up every day to color, and to grieve. What she didn't realize consciously was that her body was urging her to get in the zone *and be still for six months. Now, she designs her own coloring books, because, she says, "Coloring healed me, and I believed it could help others as well."*

In art, there is no such thing as too late.

You are never too old and never “too much.”

Art loves life experience.

Never Too Old

If you are finally doing the things you have been longing to do for a long time—like learning to sing or writing that book or painting—you may find yourself feeling regret that you have wasted so much time getting to it. You might want to say, "Where have I been all this time?" This feeling is normal, especially when you begin to experience the sheer joy of creating.

Forgive yourself, your culture, your family, and the structure of your busy life. Know that part of the joy of this newfound creativity is in part due to the contrast of the restrictions you gave into in your past. When you finally recognize the pain that being squelched caused you, you honor yourself with compassion.

Forgive yourself and be glad you found your creativity, curiosity, and passion. It's never too late to make and produce art. Some of the most passionate artists started when they were in their 50s or 60s. With art, there is no such thing as time. You are never too old, and you are never too much. Art loves life experience. Creation itself is an act of reparation and redemption.

Making art is just like
forging a new
relationship where,
in the absence of
criticism and in the
presence of trust,
you begin.

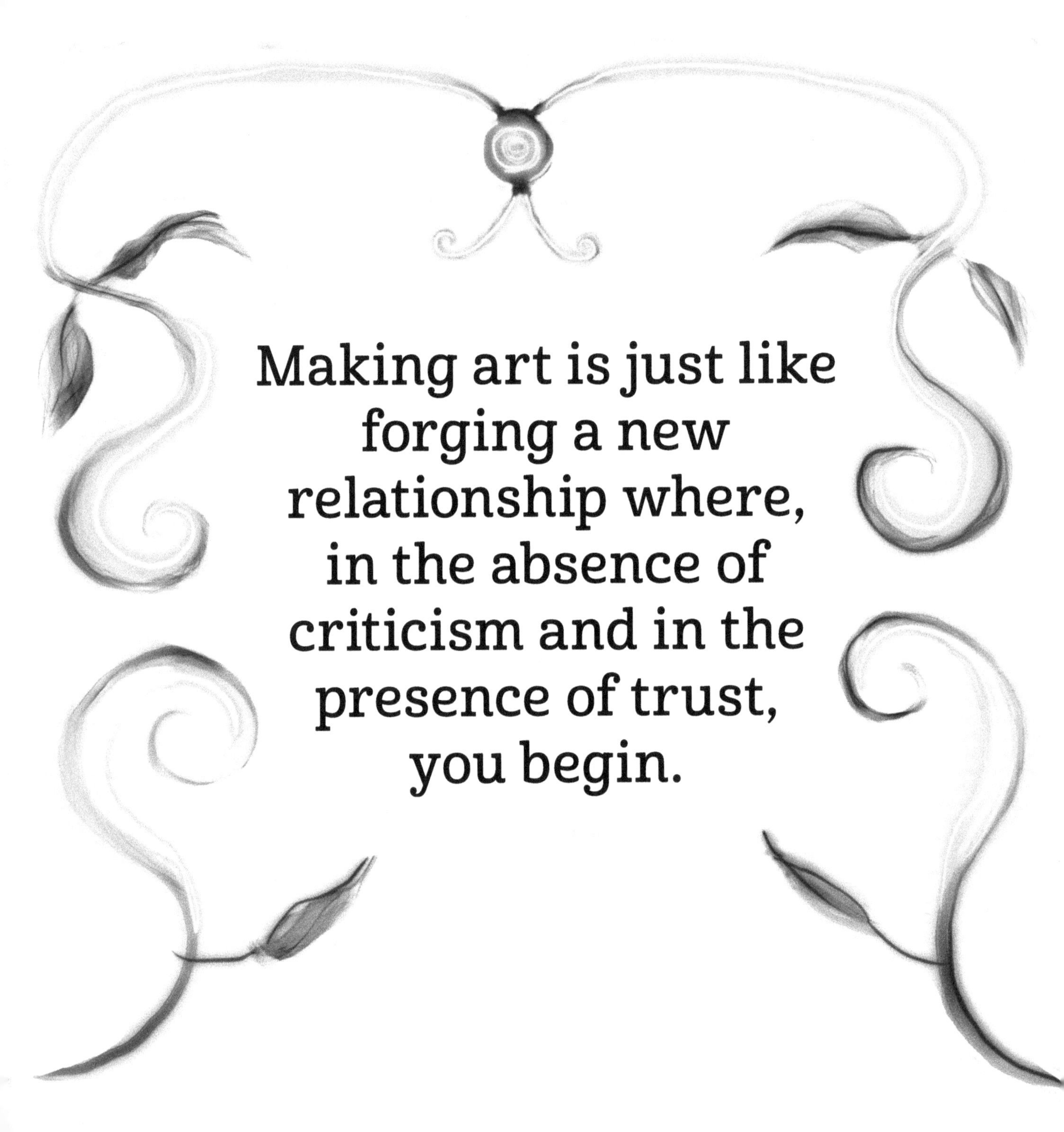

PART TWO: THE CREATIONSHIP

While creativity is often a private and personal exploration, when you tap into the relationship that is waiting for you, you will find a partnership that is a source of joy and guidance. Creativity is an opportunity to be in collaboration with an idea, sustainable guidance, and force.

The Relationship Begins

Even though the act of creating is often a solo enterprise, there are forces that are available to you for support, ideas, nourishment, and guidance. The belief that creativity must be done from your own will, discipline, and persistence is a lonely business. It is not sustainable! To experience less struggle on your path to make art and gain fulfillment, you need something I call a "creationship."

Beginning to form this trust and forge this bond is like starting a new relationship with a lover. At first, there is a spark of desire, then time is scheduled, then layers of connection happen that are made up of the synergy of both of you. One brings the skills; one brings the ability to listen and to observe. One brings the focus; the other one brings the humor. And then you trade off. After a while, there is trust. It feels warm and brings such delight to both of you. Out of the energy between the two, many things can be formed: roads, babies, houses, parties, businesses, orchards, vacation plans, ideas.

The relationship between the artist and muse is the same. Instead of creating babies and gardens, you and your muse create paintings, poetry, and portfolios filled with drawings and sketches. Be willing to accept that there is a presence bigger than you that is working through you. Let yourself feel less alone and more supported. Enter this relationship with a feeling of reverence. Feel responsible—as if you would've let down the other if you didn't show up.

Even when you are just singing a song or writing a haiku, realize how the *one thing* you are doing together begins to take form. It's as though you and the muse have a child together and the project is the child needing to be fed, changed, and watered. There is a responsibility and sense of devotion you are beginning to feel for this child-art. Your creation has its own growing energy and essence. You want to show up and make this child-art feel safe, so it can thrive.

How to Receive

Being receptive to anything in life, creative ideas and answers to your queries included, requires relaxation and a sense that you deserve everything (the good, the bad, and the neutral) that is coming to you. You must be relaxed and receptive, not hungry or striving. Maintain a sense of ease and trust that an abundance of answers, guidance, and leads are coming to you. You'll need to cultivate alertness and awareness of the signs and symbols that arrive. Have no attitude of lack! This means you need a "universe is always answering me" kind of philosophy. Subtle signs, nudges, and symbols want you to pay attention. The guidance is always there because any assistance you feel you need or would like to have is always coming your way. Remember—you're not alone. Be in touch with your muse or muses.

You'll begin to see themes, threads, or patterns. Perhaps you'll feel that you are being pulled towards something. People around you will say something that may be a clue to solving your personal puzzle. Maybe you'll click on just the right podcast or website that leads you to answers for your questions. Ideas will drop into your mind or perception. Sometimes these ideas will be so abundant that you'll pull over to the side of the road or get out of the shower and write them down.

As ideas happen more frequently, you'll feel amazed and grateful. Gratitude lights up a certain area in the brain that anxiety cannot touch! In gratitude, you feel abundant, peaceful, and taken care of. Something outside of you has your back. Gratefulness is a gateway to creativity.

In this grateful, relaxed, receptive zone where ideas are abundant, you'll need to do some dictation or note writing. Journals, an appropriate app on your smartphone, paper—keep them near! When you have set your GPS to "help me solve this," be prepared for ideas! Some ideas you will use because they are direct answers to your problems; some are trails that lead you to somewhere else. Some ideas must ripen, and others might not be useful at all.

When the flood of ideas started pouring in, I was both amazed and unnerved. Often, I was not prepared and would lose ideas because I didn't yet have a system for recording them. They would float in at inopportune moments, like when I was at a dinner event, or standing in line at the post office, or working out at the gym. Once I started to relax and saw I was being given guidance, I knew I needed to keep the proper tools nearby for receptivity. Having a belief that I deserved these gifts is what made the abundance of these ideas so amazing.

Listening

The making of art—as well as developing a healthy and thriving relationship to your creative guidance—is just like any other promising relationship where absence of criticism and presence of trust lets you begin. Here is a journal entry I made when I was first forming a relationship with my creative guidance and learning how to listen:

> *It looms above me, the white page, the screen, the canvas. Blank and ready for me to put my mark on it. Sometimes there is a word in my head, sometimes an image, sometimes a song. It beckons me; whispering or nagging and niggling, as in, "Please, I need to get born, sit still." Sometimes it is an itch, a groan inside my body that if not expressed will haunt the underpinnings of my day if it is not said or done. Now I feel there is a trusting relationship developing, and I am listening.*

You start to develop a trust between each other. You start to develop an appreciation for this new relationship. It might sound like this: "Wow. You chose to work with me. I will be a good steward of this. I will honor you, if you honor me." The relationship gets fed when you make the time for it. Consider your scheduled time to create as sacred. You must let yourself be listened to; and learn how to listen to yourself in a positive way. Be like the friend who invites you to tea in her warm and cozy kitchen by saying, "Come as you are. Come stressed, worried, overwhelmed. Just come in and sit down."

It is a thrill when you start to feel like it's not just you who is creating. It's a dance you and your support team are doing. You write a little, they write a little, you dance a little, they dance a little, you get out of the way and they do, too. "Take my hand, I am listening," you say.

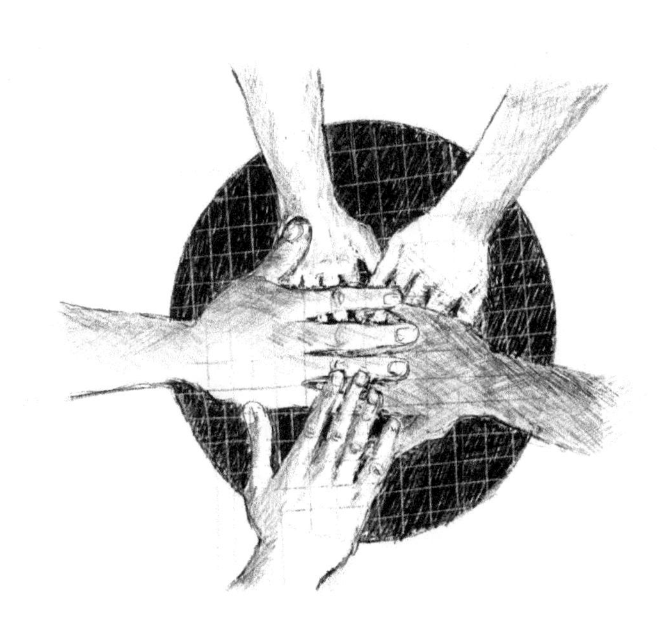

The Sound of Connection

When you engage with these forces, the practice of creating doesn't feel so isolating. There is a co-creative energy that makes creating—and life—more enjoyable, and even awe-inspiring.

It's like a loving, wise being who knows who you really are, accepts you, provides for you, and constantly has a gaze upon you. If you can receive such warmth, this being will give you all the attention you need, and you'll feel the security of a constant companion—a secret "best friend."

Expect this being to align with and support you against the forces of destruction that want to derail your efforts and inspiration. You own your source of adventure, so expand your sense of self and push out of your comfort zone to face that which is risky. Know that you yourself have a presence who can guide you when you are confused or struggling.

Sometimes, you won't know if messages coming to you are the voice of your ego (what I call the "Impeccable Artist," or, the perfectionist), or just your own enthusiasm, knowledge, and skill. Here's how you can tell the difference:

The voices of source-energy, of higher creative intelligence, are always kind. They may be playful, encouraging, or even directive at times, but there is always an absence of criticism. From this energy, you'll hear phrases like:

"Good work today."

"That was fun."

"You're tired and hungry. You can stop now." Or, ideas like:

"How about a bridge here between those two thoughts?"

"What if this object were a brighter blue?"

Or, the voice may repeat a command until you get it:

"Keep writing."

"Let's learn more about drawing."

"Stay with it; it's almost complete."

The ego, your Impeccable Artist, sounds demanding, judgmental, and snide. Demeaning. Criticizing. Worried. If the voices sound harsh, I guarantee it's not coming from your muses. This is a voice embedded with fear.

Start a practice to notice and feel the differences in these qualities of information that come to you.

Formulating the Questions

In the process of making, there will be challenges and problems for you to solve. You may ask your guidance:

"What's the next best step?"

"What is the best title for this poem?"

Just remember that when formulating a question for guidance, stay away from the negatives. Do not ask:

"What's wrong with this painting?"

"What's the problem with the lyrics here?"

"Why am I lost?"

When you ask a question from the place of lack, you open a gateway for the ego and the Impeccable Artist to inject opinions and derail you in your search. The answers will feel harsh:

"Because you're not a playwright, really."

"No. This canvas is wasted."

"You're wasting your time."

So, when looking for your solution, be specific. Ask "How?" and "What?" kinds of questions, such as:

"What's the best challenge I can give my character to solve so that he can overcome it?"

"How can I unify this painting?"

"What's a natural metaphor I can use for the feelings I'm describing here?"

"How can I bridge these two thoughts together?"

"What colors would complement this background?"

Ask, then, let go, relax and see what comes. You may get a direct answer to your question, or, you may receive information that addresses another issue that also corrects the original problem. An answer may come when you are out in the world and are not looking for it. Symbols or words with clues for you may show up and guide you to the answer you are looking for. The more you can trust your guides to lead you, the more fulfilling the process. It's a fun and often surprising dance.

Re-Quest Guidance

As in a partnership, you receive guidance and give back by being there. You want the best for each other. You are committed to the "we." Your muses have something to add to the project and so do you. You show up every day and they provide inspiration, ideas, and guidance for what you are creating together. This is not a causal relationship of commodity, but rather a give-and-take, with true partnership.

Your muses/guides/unseen forces want to help. When you are stuck, you can ask for a re-quest—which is the quest for your next step, or how to go deeper. When you ask, you will get an impulse or even direct guidance. For instance, you can ask, "How do I go deeper with this project?" Let it go and listen with the trust that you will be given a sign, nudge, or a feeling of curiosity that you must pursue.

> *Once I asked for guidance while staring at my painting. It looked like a mess. I saw a picture in my mind of different grey tones. I went back and adjusted each color with a version of its grey tone. The painting suddenly sang. It was unified.*
>
> *Once I asked for guidance before giving a hard-hitting conceptual speech. I heard, "Go through it again and look for the humor!" I did, and realized the audience could hear the new ideas better after laughing.*
>
> *Another time, with a writing project, I asked, "What's next?"*
>
> *What I heard in response was, "It's time to organize now, and stop brainstorming ideas."*

The more you trust the partnership, the more you will ask when you are stuck.
The more you ask, the more you get nudges and answers.
The more you get nudges and answers, the more trust you have.

Like a good relationship, the satisfaction keeps building. The practice of listening to the inner voices and guidance builds a feeling of trust. When the impulses, nudges, and voices feel they have been listened to, they speak a little louder and you begin to listen a little better. You start to attune to the subtle sensations in your body which tells you, "Yes. Here. Type that word, paint with this color here, follow that note."

It is so satisfying to feel that trust building. There is reverence and awe in the unseen connection between an artist and the guidance that begins to grow.

I'm not interested in discerning whether these ideas come from my brain and the skills I have developed over time, or the guidance which comes from unseen sources. What matters to my sense of creativity is the trust I have in myself and my process as it is developing. The fact that I find it pleasurable, supportive, and repeatable is a bonus. And, I keep showing up with devotion.

What works for you? Call it whatever you like—pick a concept that feels the best and supports you.

Perceiving Guidance

What if everything is guidance? What if everything you choose to experience is somehow tied synchronistically to your art? What if every click you feel drawn to listen to or read is meant to show you the way? The way the colors look on a certain morning, or the way the man at the grocery store picks out his fruit might be guidance for you. That woman you met and enjoyed talking with as you both were waiting for to-go cups of coffee might be your muse-of-the-moment!

When you see everything as guidance you will feel more of the mystery working through you. This attitude of noticing everything as a message will open you to develop your relationship to the guidance. If there are no mistakes or coincidences, why is everything not guidance? As woo-woo as it sounds, creativity is all about expanding your consciousness to make connections and see patterns. Here are some questions about this kind of connectivity:

"What about that object drew me to its form?"

"What about that song touched my heart?"

"How did that podcast I listened to inform my work today?"

"What were those ladies talking about that reminded me of my novel's main character?"

"What about the way my truck's wheels sound as I drive across the rail tracks connects to the rhythm in my music?"

"How did what I witness today inform a new way for me to see?"

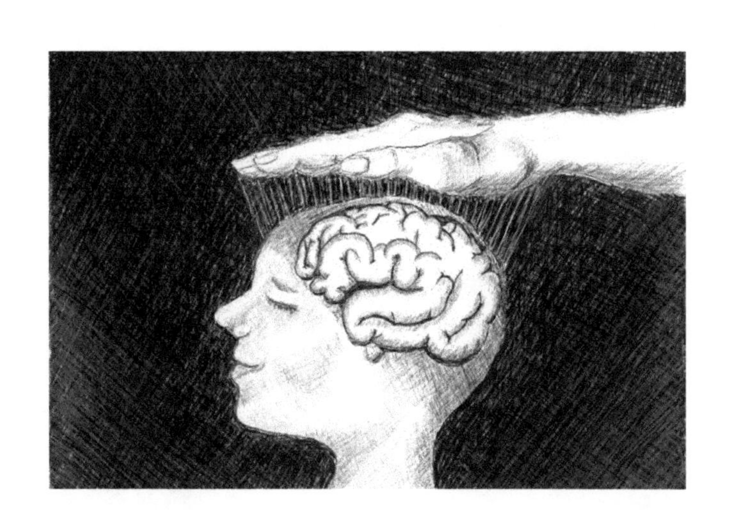

Building Safety and Trust

As in any relationship, when people feel heard, they feel safer to speak their truth. So is true with the relationship between you and your creative guidance. The practice of listening to the inner voices and guidance builds a feeling of trust. You start to attune to the subtle sensations in your body that tells you, "Yes. Here. Type that word, paint with this color here, follow that note."

There is nothing more satisfying than to feel that trust building between you. There is reverence and awe in the unseen connection between an artist and the guidance that begins to grow.

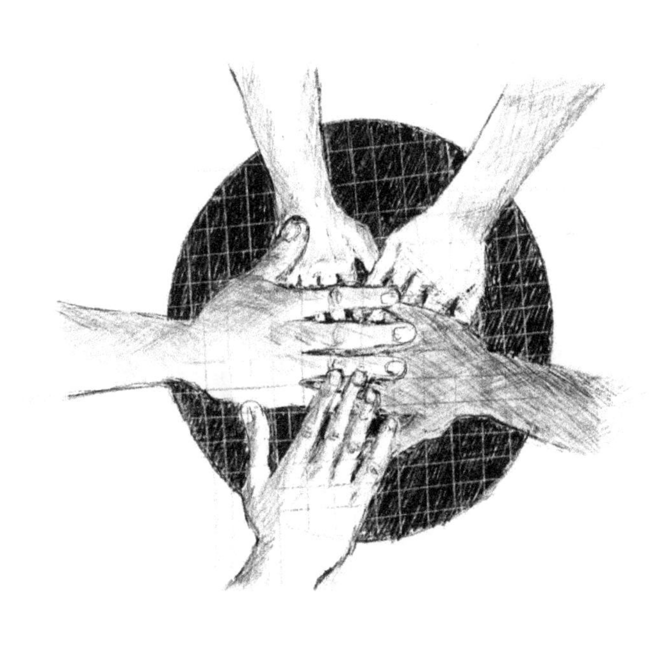

Existential Loneliness

Everyone at some point in time feels existential loneliness. It is a common human experience. When you develop a true relationship with the creator within you, your other relationships will blossom. Why? Connecting with your muses and developing trust that you are being guided makes you feel less alone and dependent on others to reassure you that you will not be abandoned or rejected. When you see that the source of your guidance is always there for you, when you sit and allow yourself to be led, you know inside that you will never be abandoned. The voices and energy are always kind and encouraging. This is the best relationship ever!

You don't need assurance from the outside world anymore. No one else can give you this kind of affirmation. Your resilience and strength create confidence and makes others feel less burdened by your needs. You can now create relationships that are kinder and more compassionate. You will experience more interdependence—and freedom to be yourself.

The paradox of the creative life is that even though creativity is often a solo activity, practicing it regularly makes you feel less alone as you develop your relationship with your guidance systems, and your muses.

Dear Muses,
I am willing.
I surrender.
I am listening.
Love,
Me

PART THREE: THE WAY IN

Maintaining a creative life requires developing skills and shifts in thinking that continually support your vision. While creativity can often be easily derailed, here are some mindsets that can hold and sustain you in helping you pave the way for more creative support and less struggle.

Know your intention.
Take some steps.
Hand it over to
the mystery.

The Chamber

Here is what I often hear my clients say when they claim they must create or find the perfect environment in order to begin their *one thing*:

"I will paint as soon as I redesign my guest room."

"As soon as I clean out the kids' rooms, I will start writing."

"When we finally clean out the garage, I'll create a wood shop."

Waiting for the perfect exterior environment is a fancy form of procrastination. If everyone waited for the perfect writing studio or place to practice dance moves, nobody would ever do a damn thing. The idea that you can't make things until the environment is perfect is a limiting thought and it keeps you from realizing your potential and your creations.

The true perfect place is in your imagination. Access your imagination through your mind by concentrating on designing your internal place of creation. Decorate it with feelings of safety and inspiration. This is like a great summer camp you can keep returning to in any season; a place where you always thrive. Your imagination design studio is also a portable workspace. I think of mine as a chamber. Others have conceived a geodome, a tunnel, a tent, a yurt, a cave, a pyramid, a sanctuary. All of these are places in your energy field where you can receive inspiration and explore ideas. My chamber is like the house of a hobbit—a round room with ancient windowpanes, and a fine polished desk that gleams with light that streams through the leaded windows.

The most important thing about your imagined studio of creation is the good feeling you'll have when you're in there. You'll create good feelings so the pleasure of returning to your imagined space is always a safe homecoming. When you do this, you are in a new state of being. This new state is the feeling you create in body, mind, and spirit in order to receive the wave-like frequency of a higher nature, something bigger than yourself. It is safe way of being, a place where all kinds of positive things can happen. You've created your own think tank, where the first rule is that of safety. It is here where you are safe to brainstorm in a judgement-free zone. All ideas are welcome, and all exploration is accepted. Think of non-judgement in your creative environments as the Miracle-Gro™ for your plants.

Like grandma's kitchen, every time you sit at that table in your imagination, you are greeted with warmth and acceptance. Something good is always baking in the oven. It smells delicious and you know you will soon be served something warm and tasty. Your stories are heard, your art is seen, and you are always nourished. This is an internal place where the muses come to find you. It is where you create the internal environment so you can be more flexible in the external environments you happen to work in. When you create a luscious internal space for yourself, a place where you can explore and expand, a place where there are no external demands on you—you can work anywhere. You are a mobile unit!

Even when I'm working in a coffee shop or a library, my chamber is a warm and inviting place—an environment inside of me that is a pleasurable and safe place of inspiration and exploration. I know that when I enter my "chamber time," I am always safe and loved.

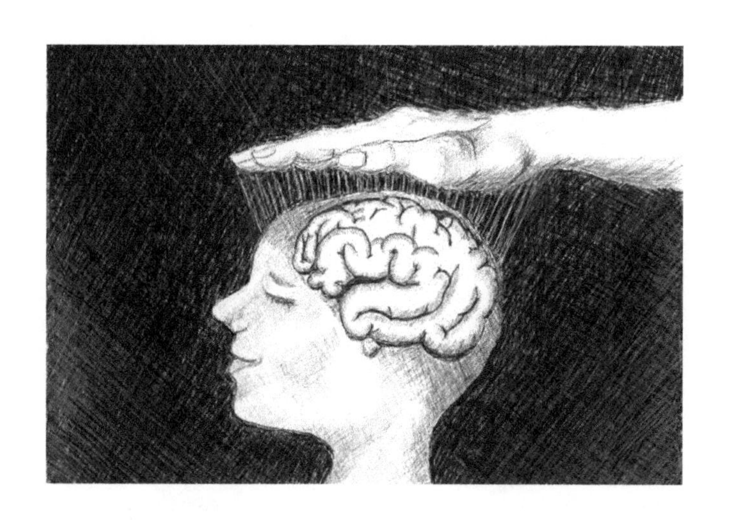

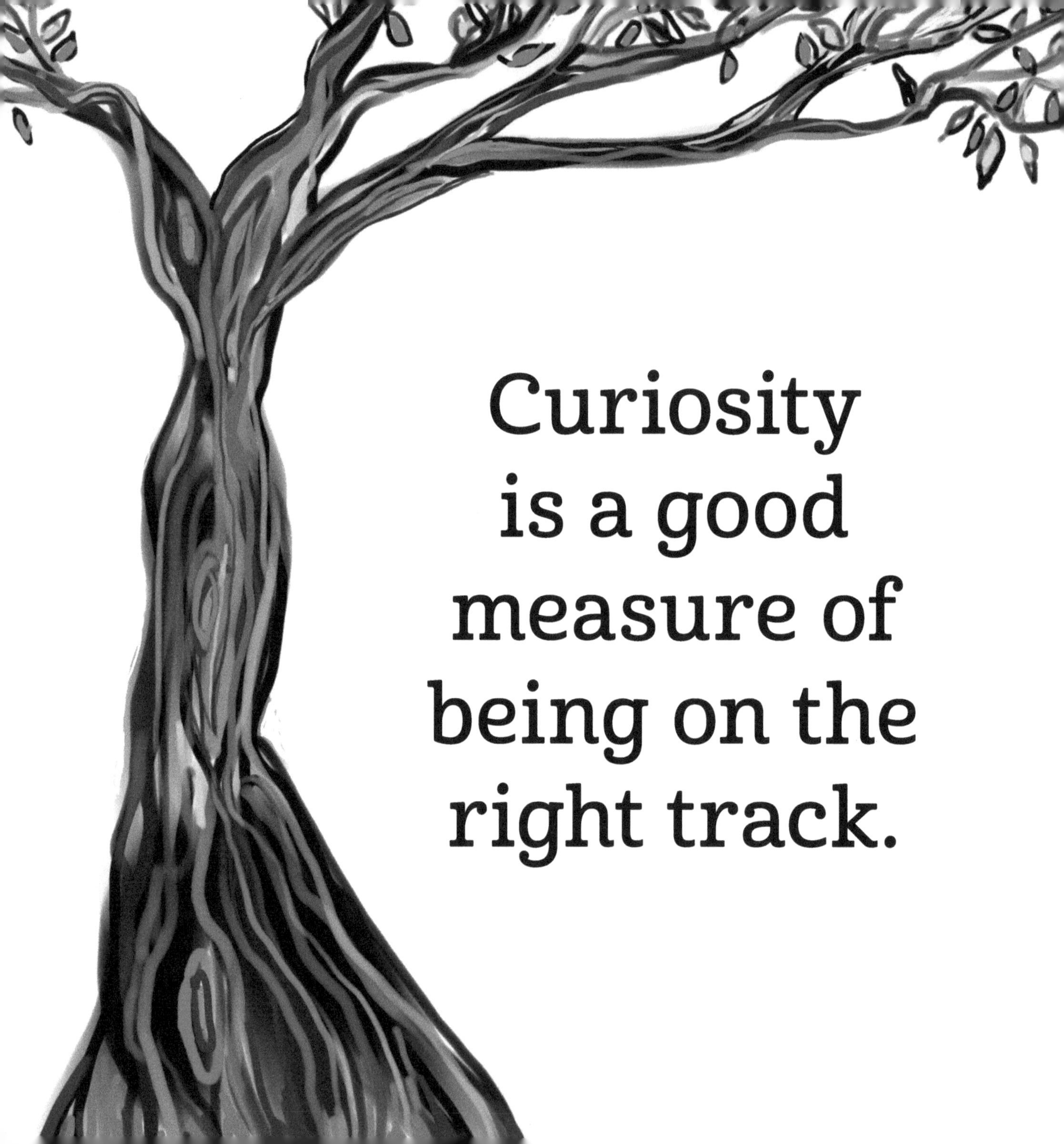
Curiosity
is a good
measure of
being on the
right track.

Curiosity: The Dorothy Story

Have you ever met someone who inspired you so completely with their unique perspective and "beingness" that it changed your life? Here is what happened for me on the day I was invited to a weekly art workshop given by a woman in her home.

I found my human muse in a dusty bungalow in Burbank. I was greeted with the humble smell of fresh butcher paper laid across antique wooden tables, classical music and quiet murmurings of students busy with their hands. Sunlight settled lazily across the old wooden floor, which signaled I had arrived in the sweet spot of home.

Dorothy Cannon stood there shining...with her silver hair twisted up and her radiant eyes belying her 87 years.

"Welcome! And what are you curious about making today?"

There were blocks of clay, paints, charcoals, oil pastels, pen and ink, papier mâché, and printmaking. Dorothy had turned her deceased sister's house into a workshop space where women of all ages came to create. The living room was for making, the kitchen was lined with pots ready for the kiln. A potting wheel waited in the backyard where, if your curiosity nudged, Dorothy would offer the most minimalistic instruction, as if she were a creative monk.

"Keep your hands and mind still."

Always some new visual inspiration was proffered; a model posing in a corner, a fresh bowl of fruit, a vase of flowers.

"When you look, what do you feel? Draw that feeling," she's said, as if your inner nature were your wisdom and your curiosity were the secret to the universe.

She never gave me advice except, "Do not go to art school." The environment, she told me, would shut a creative down and cause them to lose trust in themselves. The time and energy it would take to undo the restrictions those environments created were too much work when you could be using it to create art. She believed you would know the next resource you needed, the next information, the next experience, if you trusted yourself. You would find your own way. Your body would tell you.

The safe environment she created was like Miracle-Gro™ for those of us who were lucky enough to be under her tutelage. We blossomed under that nurturance.

Novice or experienced, all drank from the Dorothy cup. Everyone looked alive; eyes shiny and faces soft. Folks were quick to laugh and happy to encourage. Women trusted their own inner urges and those of each other. We were making unique art; inspired and fresh. We were like the Bloomsbury group, we were the Fauvists, we were 1920s Paris Bohemians and I had stumbled upon my tribe in Burbank, circa 1983.

I finished a painting and stepped back. She appeared at my side and gently removed the canvas from the easel with, "Marvelous. Do another one." Words of "good" or "bad," were not heard. She was embodying freedom from the addiction for others' approval, including hers. Not interested in perfection here, all in the doing.

With her gnarled hands, she handled each painting, drawing, or pot as if it belonged in the Smithsonian. "She's working with animals. Isn't that marvelous?" Not that the object was marvelous, but that the student was turning what was invisible (a longing, a curiosity) into something real. As if she could see that everyone had a God-given, inalienable, cellular imperative to express by creating. That was the "marvelous" thing.

Like a midwife, she had the ability to perceive obstacles to a smooth delivery (usually culturally or familial). All she required was a creative implement and the spark of one's nature to usher it into being.

As was her nature, she passed away simply and without fanfare. I believe that besides her being my true muse, she had also dropped her midwifery magic into me on her way out. Yesterday, I observed myself coaching a client with, "What have you been curious about?" ...as if asking it would reveal the secret of the universe.

Anyone I have ever shared this story with wanted to know more about Dorothy. She suffered from tuberculosis (TB) and lived in a sanitorium and then with family for 15 years until she got her strength back. Whether she was lying in bed recovering or working with groups, she did art every day. When she was strong enough, she created art classes for children and for adults in her sister's home. She charged a nominal drop-in fee, and anyone was free to come anytime during the weekly hours (two-hour sessions at a time) she kept her studio open. Her lungs were compromised all her life due to the TB. Later, due to macular degeneration of her eyes, being close to blindness, she still continued to do art every day, moving into clay sculptures.

She held her workshops up until one week before she died—with her nephew and a mentee of hers by her side. She left six nieces and nephews. Her nephew Jay manages The Art of Dorothy Cannon, a website where you can see her art (www.dorothycannon.com).

The Spirit of Discovery

Being an artist means you are always gathering, stretching, and fueling yourself in a nourishing way. You feed yourself with thoughts of creativity just as you feed yourself breakfast, lunch, dinner. When you follow your curiosities in the real world, you will be more attuned to follow your inner nudges when you're in your chamber. You'll develop a sensitivity to subtle yesses and gentle nos. The more you listen and act on guidance from your physical senses, the more you'll trust yourself as a creative human being.

When you give yourself full reign to explore areas that are new to you, the more excited and fulfilled you'll feel. It's like the difference between traveling to a new city and staying in your hotel room reading a book versus walking about, talking to people, and taking in the culture (art, food, music, scenery, smells, weather, etc.) of a space that is new to you. You feed yourself and grow your confidence when you push out of your comfort zone. In the movie "Harold and Maude," Maude said: "Otherwise, you got nothing to talk about in the locker room." It's my favorite movie.

It's the spirit of discovery that you admire in others who push themselves beyond themselves. It's not really about passion; it's about discovery and curiosity. That's what their internal radiance is about.

I met a woman, Susan, who embodied this spirit of discovery. She was 72 years of age and looked like she was in her 50s. She did something new every week, and explained, "My motto is 'if not now, then when?'"

Susan and I had both signed up for an all-day storytelling boot camp. Eleven of us would be given a writing prompt in the morning and then we'd write, re-write, and rehearse a personal story during the day in preparation for the performance of it in the evening. We were all doing something that was scary and pushed our edges of discomfort. We bonded as a group as dopamine flooded our brains. Susan had never performed before and was terrified to read her story. However, the story she wrote, and the way she performed it, was by far the most hilarious one of all. I believed that it was this spirit for discovery that she had developed in herself that set her apart from the rest.

Have you ever taken a workshop or class in the creative arts (painting, storytelling, writing, songwriting, dance, speaking, figure-drawing)? Do you feel lifted from challenging yourself? Do you relish in the learning of new skills? Do you enjoy pushing yourself out of your comfort zone in the company of others doing the same?

The Impeccable Artist

You, like all creatives, have said, "It doesn't matter what I do. No one cares anyway. There is already too much noise in the world." Do you recognize this voice? Well, you certainly might, especially if you have a creative project in mind that you are not doing. Everyone has the disempowering voice of an Impeccable Artist inside. This voice is the reason people never get to their *one thing*. It causes them to justify never starting anything of true creative worth. It's now time to call out your Impeccable Artist in full light.

The Impeccable Artist in you was formed by outside ideas/beliefs embedded in the culture and society you've lived in all your life. Your Impeccable Artist is made up of a culmination of your creative wounds—harms caused by the people in your life that dashed your joy, other artists you admire and think you can't emulate, and, the general rules regarding what art should and shouldn't be. The Impeccable Artist's operating principle is based on some idealized vision of perfect art. That vision of perfect art doesn't exist in reality!

This figment of perfection is in everybody, especially when it comes to making art. Like the ego, and the voice of fear, you might think that the unrealistic standard of what is a "worthy product" was invented to keep you from making a fool out of yourself. "What a waste of time. You produced nothing of value here." But here's the deal: the perfect artist does no work and offers nothing but criticism. The Impeccable Artist doesn't have any fresh ideas, nor is it ever willing to get dirty hands while doing creative work.

Mr. Impeccable Artist is like the Little Leaguer's father (who has no experience in baseball) sitting in the bleachers and hollering at his child over the coach's authority.

Ms. Impeccable Artist is like a gallery owner who has all the right ideas about art, and what you "should" or "shouldn't" do with it. She believes that you should (can you tell that "should" is her favorite word?) have learned this already and you should already have been making money.

The Impeccable Artist doesn't believe in the idea of trial and error; nor do they believe in muses because, "That's too woo-woo."

Any Impeccable Artist will say, "You are either born an artist, or not."

All Impeccable Artists don't believe in reinvention; everything should have already been in place the first time. Your need to paint or dance is a waste of time.

Impeccable Artists are the voices of a culture that only values money-making pursuits. "What difference does it make if it doesn't make money?"

The sounds of the Impeccable Artists' chorus are only the culmination of your ego's deepest fears, doubts, and insecurities. This chorus will criticize you, compare you to others, and demean you. Each voice wants to sabotage your most genuine of efforts and squelch your soul's calling. Notice that this chorus never actually does anything other than sing an anthem of negativity. The group observes from over your shoulder and sings petty, atonal melodies that are hurtful and judgmental.

You recognize your own Impeccable Artist by the way it makes you feel in your gut—namely contracted and tight. Mine sometimes makes me feel nauseous. Through the eyes of my Impeccable Artist, my writings or efforts to make graphic art always seem meaningless.

While the muses speak to you in whispers and nudges, the voice of your Impeccable Artist is snide, sarcastic, or, if threatened, will shout and holler commands. The Impeccable Artist has opinions about how you are not good enough and what the best use of your time should be, like that judgmental family member everyone simply tolerates at Thanksgiving.

While everybody's creative wounds are different, the focus of each Impeccable Artist is similar. It is primarily interested in comparing your work unfavorably to those of other people, or to point out the judgment you will most certainly receive if your work was to ever come to light.

Your Impeccable Artist wants to shame you for every creative impulse you have, often by manufacturing disastrous imaginary future scenarios.

Disabling Your Impeccable Artist

The Impeccable Artist has the capability of disempowering the most accomplished of artists. One of the prerequisites of being an artist is learning to disable your Impeccable Artist. Every single creative has one. Nobody is immune. Having an internal Impeccable Artist is the price you pay for reaching outside of your comfort zone. Like a bully on the playground, the Impeccable Artist can be suppressed, but never banished for they are always there. However, they can be worked with and managed—maybe even put in a time-out or two. There is a powerful rush of determination and a declaration of your own self-agency when you can bring to light and rein in your Impeccable Artist. You do this by training yourself to hear the subtle put-downs and learn to deal with them in a constructive way that works.

Here are seven words, all starting with the letter "C" (and the sound "see!") I've developed in my work with artists that will put your Impeccable Artist in its place: Catch, Challenge, Compassion, Compromise, Call out, Chide, Curse. Now, here's how they work in a dialogue between your own Impeccable Artist (IA) and you.

Catch: Catch them in the act. Like any bully or thief, the minute they know you are on to them, they will be forced to watch themselves more closely or change tactics.

IA: "You will never be a real painter."

You: "I see you're at it again—just as I'm starting to paint. Look! I'm painting. It's real."

Challenge: Some artists like to threaten these voices with a challenge which gives the message that if the IA continues to persist, they will show them!

IA: "You are wasting your time on writing a song today?"

You: "Go ahead, just try to stop me. Here, let me sing a verse to you!"

Compassion: The IA wants to keep you safe from judgement or criticism. Connect to its pure motive of acceptance.

IA: "There is nothing elegant here. This painting looks like it belongs in a college dorm."

You: "I know you're trying to keep from making a fool of myself, but I am going to paint with these intense colors. Dorm room—get ready for some art."

Compromise: Like with children, when you give them a job, they stop whining. Give the IA a job. Assign your IA to help with punctuation while you're editing your poem. Let yours clean your brushes at the end of a day. Tell it to sweep the floor after you're finished carving the statue. Tell it to watch you do whatever you're creating, but it may not run the show.

IA: "You don't know what you're doing here."

You: "Tell ya what, I'll make a bargain with you. When I sign my name on this, I'll let you do the lettering."

Call out: All bullies hate being exposed by being disciplined in public. It makes them feel foolish. The more aware you are of your IA's rude comments, the more you can expose it for the bully it is.

IA: "You aren't as good of a singer as Mike is."

You: "And you should know because you're no singer yourself!"

Chide: Just like their hatred of being called out, bullies do not like to be laughed at. When real awareness of their crazy-making comments is exposed, you can laugh at them.

IA: "This is so typical of you, wasting your time on this when you should be doing something worthwhile."

You: "This is so typical of you—criticizing me when you could be doing something worthwhile. Bahahaha!"

Curse: Sometimes only cursing will get the message across. If you are forceful enough, you will feel determination coursing through your body—and anchoring your own power. You are more powerful than this cardboard cut-out voice.

IA: "You are not actually going to try to publish that story, are you?"

You: "Hell yes, you asshole! I am going to fucking publish this damn story."

Beware: Your IA may shift and change tactics once it knows you mean business. It may start to get on the same artistic project with you and start a new tactic: "shoulding" you to death:

"You should review how the masters accomplished this kind of painting."

"You should be working on the introduction now."

"You should be revising those lyrics."

"You should be: taking out your trash / washing your dishes / pulling weeds / cooking dinner now…you should always do your creative work after you take care of other parts of your life."

Some of the should the IA offers may be decent suggestions, but you will know true guidance by the tone you hear. If it is harsh and critical, it is never good guidance—it's the IA. You can accept the "should," but remember, you always have a choice.

The Difference Between Ego and Pure Consciousness

What once was coming from a pure place of creative imagination can easily be derailed by the voices of your Impeccable Artist or ego. Those voices are fueled by the energy of fear and lack. Watch out—your ego can hide behind high standards and so-called powerful stances.

How do you tell the difference between these different energies?

It is in the quality of the doing.

There is a quality of force when you are acting from the ego. It sounds like this: "I gotta get this done." Or, "I'm going to be the best at this."

So, the doing is stressful. The ego wants its fulfillment from the thing that's already done, and done perfectly, so it feels the need to use force. When such force is at play, there will be a feeling of missing something. You'll feel antagonism, perhaps pressure, about time. Perhaps you'll direct your irritation at other people who you may be angry or frustrated with, those who are easy targets.

Your ability to create comes from the pure place of your innocent intention. There is no force. There is an energy stream that feels powerful—not forceful. You can be deeply focused in the flow state, and from the outside, it may look like you're cranking out the vision of your art with intensity, but your internal feeling is of enjoyment and enthusiasm. This is an empowered feeling, but it's also enjoyable, and you will have a sense of enthusiasm. (By the way, the word "enthusiasm" came from the definition, "possessed of God.") There is no feeling of missing anything, except you may feel that you've lost track of time. There will be no "shoulds" present.

While in the act of doing, you'll know you are coming from a place of ego when you feel stress. When you notice that you are stressed, you must also know that it signals the beginning of change. Through your awareness of something undesired (such as stress), you can shift your perspective. Awareness is the beginning of this kind of positive change.

Here are some questions to ask yourself to assess your state of doing:

"What is my state right now?"
"Where do I feel tension in my body?"
"What pressure do I feel while I'm working?"
"What do I think 'should' be different?"
"While working, do I notice that I am having fun?"
"Did I lose track of time?"

Voluntary Transformation

Engaging your creativity changes you. It is like a rainstorm that you willingly walk into and through, without a raincoat or an umbrella, knowing you will be changed in an unforeseen way. When you make an agreed upon appointment with yourself and your muses (which you may define as source, angels, your higher self, God, a god, the universe, or just a great, good thing that's impossible to name) to begin a practice of creating, know that your self-doubts and fears (disguised as the ego or the Impeccable Artist) will come up to greet you. It's the way of creativity. If you stay in the rain, accept it, and bear the discomfort, this process will give you a cleaned-out version of yourself, with even more life force than before. It's why you feel so calm and well-used after making. Like after a storm which seems destructive and violent, the aftermath of drenched earth becomes rich and more verdant. It's as if you can imagine and feel the life force pushing its way up from waters left by the deluge.

So too with creativity. Whatever form of creative storm you find yourself moving towards or in, know you will be changed. Here are some questions to ask while you're in that rainstorm:

"Who will I be at the end of this?"

"How will the alchemy of water change me?"

And, here are some possible outcomes of withstanding the deluge of a creative storm:

- Confidence, pride, delight, resilience
- Better memory retention and recall
- Feelings of being stronger, fresher, funnier, braver, kinder, and even sexier
- Freedom, peace, satisfaction, and/or fulfillment
- Enhanced curiosity, passion, openness, focus, trust
- A sense of vitality, authenticity, and/or new awareness
- A stronger connection to your spirit

Here's what you may experience less of:

- Resistance
- Judgement
- Stress
- Self-doubt
- Fear
- Loneliness
- Victimization

The changes that occur after you've been able to express yourself in creative ways are almost always for the better. If you experience any negative reaction, give it time. Creativity—once expressed—has a magical way of ironing out any wrinkles, even if it takes a while.

Banish the Word "Should"

Welcome to your "should show."

The "should show" has no place in creativity. What everyone else is doing has nothing to do with you. Comparison is the thief of joy.

According to the Online Etymology Dictionary, the word "should" originated around the year 1200 to define "obligation." Obligation is all about black-and-white, all-or-nothing thinking. Perfectionism. Rigidity. Following trends. Over-researching instead of doing. Fear is always in the driver's seat when it comes to obligation, and its destination always is a "should show."

In fact, to work with the natural propensity you may have to "should" all over the place, a powerful exercise to counteract your "shouldisms" is to say, "I should be exactly where I am." And, "I should be doing exactly what I'm doing; my project is exactly where it should be." Saying these sentences doesn't make you lazy; it's just the opposite. The more acceptance you bring to the present moment, without resistance, the more energy you have available to you.

So, how are you "shoulding" on yourself?

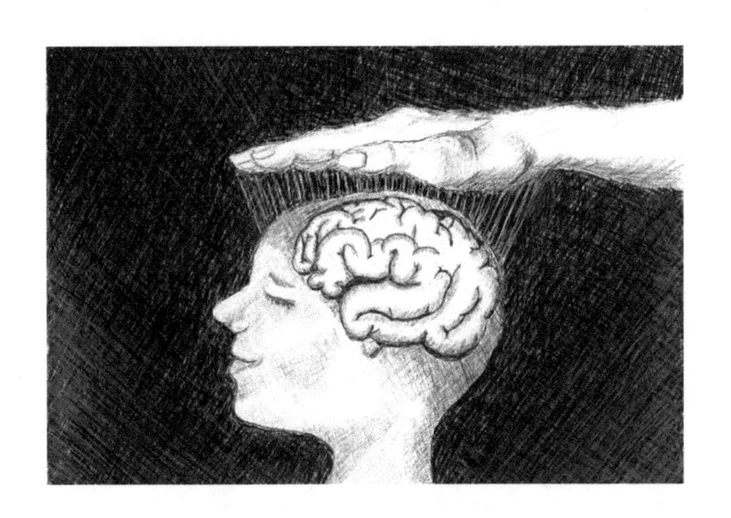

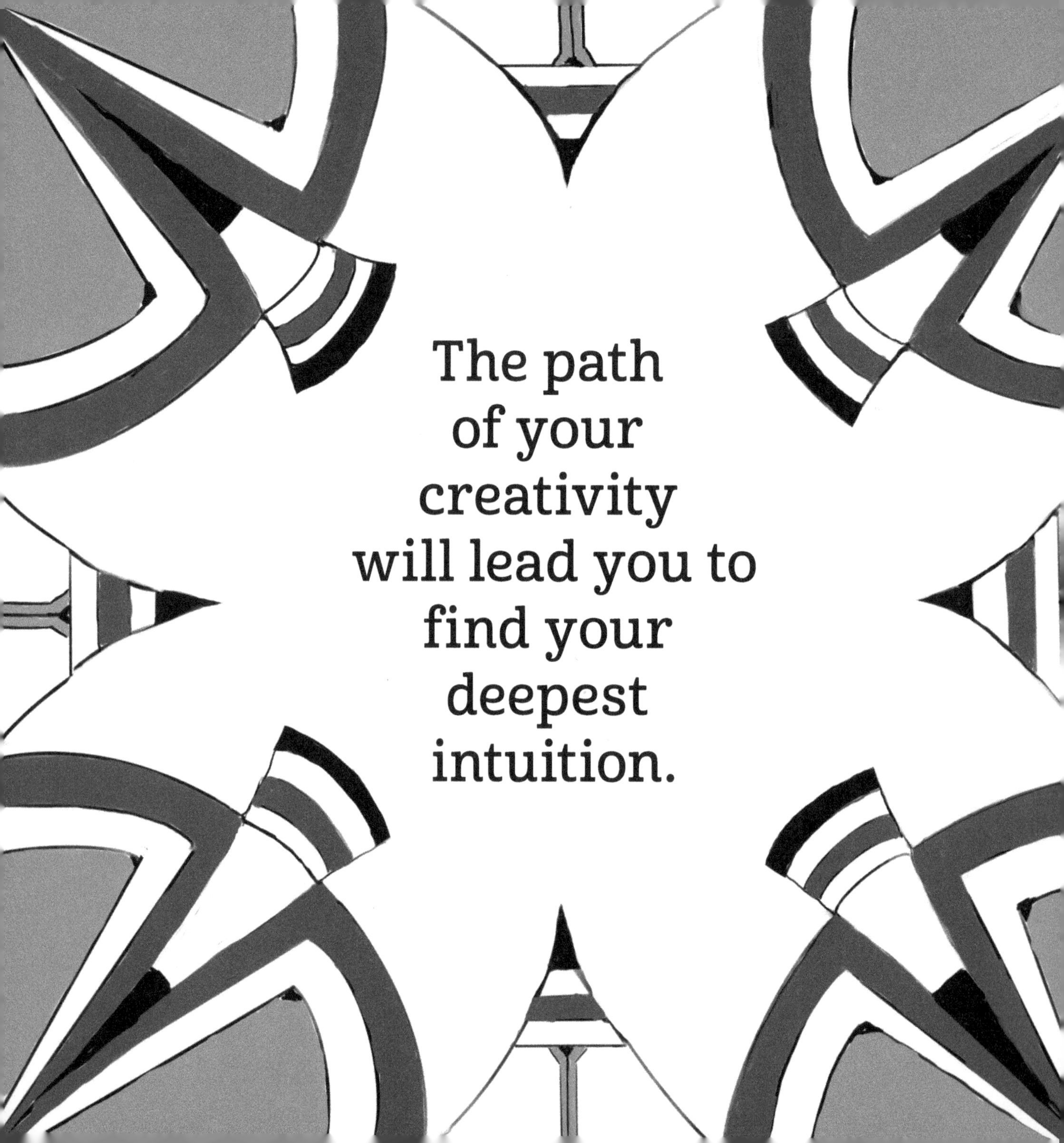
The path
of your
creativity
will lead you to
find your
deepest
intuition.

Free the Monkeys

The opposite of the word "fun" is not "work." It's the word "should." All animals and children play. It's natural. Especially in America, people think that in order to be good and valuable grownups, they must work all the time. They must have discipline to contribute to society and make money. The results produced from such discipline are societally sanctioned; they define people in terms of commodity and status. The "shoulds" kill humanity.

In contrast, creativity is all about a having a playful attitude. All those rules and beliefs wreak havoc on your ability to have access to your playfulness. Creativity is all about accessing and using your playfulness. No wonder Americans have heart attacks, high blood pressure, and other ills at astounding rates. After a lifetime of "the shoulds," the body wears down. There are diets and medications that reduce blood pressure; there are diet/exercise plans that may reduce heart attacks. I propose that if people were put on a diet that included play for at least one month, it would improve everyone's health. What might everyday acts of carefree play look like?

- Roll down a grassy hill and get some green stains on your pants
- Swim naked in the ocean—risk arrest
- Wrestle with your family and get your kids all wound up before bedtime
- Make a fairy garden with found objects
- Make love for hours and then nap; share dreams; waste the day being a heathen
- Laugh with your friends in the restaurant to inspire other diners to follow suit
- Spend all Sunday painting one wall in your house in a bold color
- Make a good memory with someone by cooking together, going for a walk, or laying on a blanket under the stars
- Pick up rocks and spend the rest of the day placing them in your yard
- Experiment in the kitchen with foods you aren't familiar with

- Take yourself out to the hardware store and think up untraditional usages for the items you see

What I'm proposing is a delicious effervescence—available to everyone through play. Play asks that you do have a regard for the certain rules in our society—such as the ones that keep people out of harm's way. Allow yourself permission to engage in playtime, out of the blue, like you did as a kid, before the "should" took over. This is a freedom that will make you feel younger and healthier and happier. It will also free you in your art, when you allow it.

Dignify the Monkeys, Not Punish Them

You, like most of us, are often imprisoned in a jail of your own making. What is this jail? Its bars are formed by these questions:

"What am I supposed to be?"

"What is acceptable?"

"What is normal?"

"What is respectable?"

How do you get out of that jail? The keys are contained in your answers to these questions:

"What delights me?"

"What would I do if nobody was watching?"

"Where is joy found here?"

"What would I do if I saw this from a child's perspective?"

"What does my body love about this moment?"

"What would I let my body do if there were no restrictions?"

Play and fun have a bad rap. American culture seems to have always valued the serious. We've had it all wrong. In my opinion, play is a more enlightened state of being than we are domesticated to consider. When someone is playful, they have a relationship to possibility. Think of the phrase: "Anything can happen!" It brings on a state of play that insists on being present and living in the moment. It commands you to be on the alert for that which delights and elevates yourself as well as others. When you live in the moment, you vibrate at a higher frequency. This state is what attracts others to you.

There is an energy of non-judgement and opportunity amongst playmates that speaks something like this: "Your spirit and mine can collide and make something together." These playmates experience freedom from worry. Play is also important when you're alone—it reveals different kinds of creative insights—some of which are deeper than you'll get while spending playtime with another person. Just remember, you cannot be playful and worried at the same time. When you play, there is an openness and willingness for ideas to form.

In the play zone, expansive questions naturally come out of the energy of play, and the questions sound like: "Why not?" and "What if?" and "What's possible?" When you are under the umbrella of play, it's impossible to ask what's wrong, why something won't work, or who is judging or comparing you.

To increase
your "wins"
adopt a
willingness
to "fail."

Make Some Really Bad Messes

There is a powerful freedom in giving yourself permission to make some bad art. It breaks the back of your Impeccable Artist who'll be so upset while watching you do it. On the other hand, your muses love it! They can reach you when you get those restrictive, heady thoughts out of the way.

Once you give yourself full permission to make a complete mess, to be the worst painter in the United States, or to write the junkiest novel in the English-speaking world, you set yourself free.

Allowance of messiness, mistakes and mediocrity teaches you to fly and gives you permission to explore. It's a portal for innovation. Through bad, you find your way to unique. Like a healthy think tank, you create an environment that feels free and honors the sheer pleasure of the process. You find yourself becoming playful, which is the muses' favored state in which to find you.

The mess you make is a fertile training ground for perfectionists. The irony is that you will see that out of chaos can come…unique new styles, and fresh voices. The irony is when you allow yourself mediocrity, you can explore new horizons. When you allow yourself to be a beginner, you are on the road to new freedoms and…more fun.

Creative messes are like compost. They brim with the light and heat of life; they promise fertile possibility. In fact, the more you make messes, the more you'll see the value in making them. Really shitty messes make good second drafts, and often send you unintentionally into the 'happy accident' zone. Keep playing in the mud. There usually is some gold in the muck.

What's Already Working

In positive psychology, the focus is on strength, not brokenness. I believe the best approaches to your creativity are in your attention to what's already working for you.

You may not possess the drawing skills you'd like in order to do the painting, but you know you can push yourself to learn new things step-by-step. You possess a curiosity and a willingness to learn. You happen to be great with color, for instance, so the way you get them to bounce off each other is what makes your paintings work. You are also interested in learning a little more about drawing because of what you already possess in the color department.

I believe you keep coming back to your art when you can see what you have brought to the table from other disciplines. Ask yourself:

"What am I already good at?"

"What strengths do I already possess that I can bring to my creativity?"

"When was a time that I stretched myself to learn areas I was curious about that further strengthened what talents and strengths I already had?"

Happy Flow

If you show up enough in *the zone* or the flow state, you are going to want to be there more often. Sure, you'll be learning and growing, but being in this state just plain feels good. In fact, it is a delicious sensation—it is as though healthy energy is flowing through your body and cleaning you out.

When you lose track of time, you are in the flow state.

Think of the times when you've lost track of time. Maybe you were on vacation, perhaps you were making love and connecting, or you were having a wonderful conversation with a friend. That's what the flow state feels like. When you are in flow, you are focused on the project and your mind is not in stress mode. You relax. You are open to inspiration, and inspiration feels good.

It also means that your brain has slid out of the beta wave state and you're in the alpha or theta state which is your place of creativity and connectivity with the divine.

Can you be happy doing what is uncomfortable? Yes.

Can your happiness increase when you are in flow state, doing what you love? Absolutely!

Gentling

While learning and trying new things is fun, it's difficult to start new things. It's not easy to commit to a project. It's hard to show up every day doing things you are not good at yet.

How would you give guidance and encouragement to a child who is trying valiantly but missing the mark? Chances are you'd say, "You are such a winner for showing up and learning. It's hard to try new things, but you are not afraid." You'd remind them of a time when they'd conquered another skill but struggled at first.

I call this "gentling." Gentle yourself when the going gets tough. Encourage yourself when you are lost. Remind yourself of other times when you've struggled with projects or gathered new skills that you did in fact learn and you did in fact master.

> *I must gentle myself every week when I'm learning to dance salsa. I can never remember the damn steps. I gentle myself by saying, "Look at the way you just keep showing up for these lessons. And good for you. Your body will learn. You've learned hard things before."*

Don't punish yourself or make judgements because you're not good yet. Treat yourself with the respect you would show a child who is struggling.

Be kind.

Talk nice.

Be gentle.

Surprise as Evidence

What's more delicious than experiencing the feeling of being a conduit for creativity? You're out of the way of yourself. Words, movements, and images flow through you. Time means nothing. Your body loses all rigidity. You feel an energy flow—a life force—and you know you are being used for good: To make beauty, to make something functional, to tell a human story that connects yourself to others.

What's really astounding is when you stop, step back, review your creation...and you feel surprised. You may say, "I wrote that?" or, "That came through me?"

You know that you yourself (or, your ego self with all the big important ideas) did not make that creation. It was done through you. These surprises are evidence of your alignment with source energy, and it is one of the best highs ever. No mind-altering substances needed!

Choosing True Fulfillment

There are four types of behaviors that affect the quality of your life, as well as the quality of your creativity. These behaviors begin at the most negative level and rise:

1. When you do things that don't feel good and are not healthy or fulfilling. These behaviors have been repeated for so long, they are now a part of your identity. They have evolved by being repeated, such as chasing immediate rewards that became full-blown addictions. This is the most difficult behavior to change. Instead of choosing to start the *one thing* you chose to do other things that you felt would please people. It felt terrible and there was a cost to it. The result is that you feel bad about yourself and have anxiety and despair about abandoning your dreams. You see yourself as a loser.
2. Doing things that feel good in the moment, but they are not healthy or fulfilling. You chase immediate rewards that are temporary. You sometimes play a little at doing your *one thing*, but mostly, you do what is easy, comfortable, and is approved of by the family system. You don't experience the growth that choosing a regular creative practice brings. You do experience anxiety about it, but it's just easier to go with the flow and do it only when you feel in the mood. You think of yourself as a dilettante—a dabbler—who is not very serious about their *one thing*.
3. You do things that don't feel good at first, but they are healthy and fulfilling. The more you do these things; they start to feel good. Choosing creative behaviors consistently over time will create a life filled with true happiness. Every day, you choose to create time and energy to do your *one thing*. You experience the discomfort of learning new things and pushing through. You have the hard conversations with your family and learn to set boundaries that allow time to create. You are proud of your process despite the discomfort. You think of yourself as a committed creative.

4. You do things that feel good and are healthy and fulfilling. This is living the good life—the life that supports your dreams. It's a confident life, a whole life, a no-regrets life. You show up in your creativity every day and it is something you feel great about. You think of yourself as an artist.

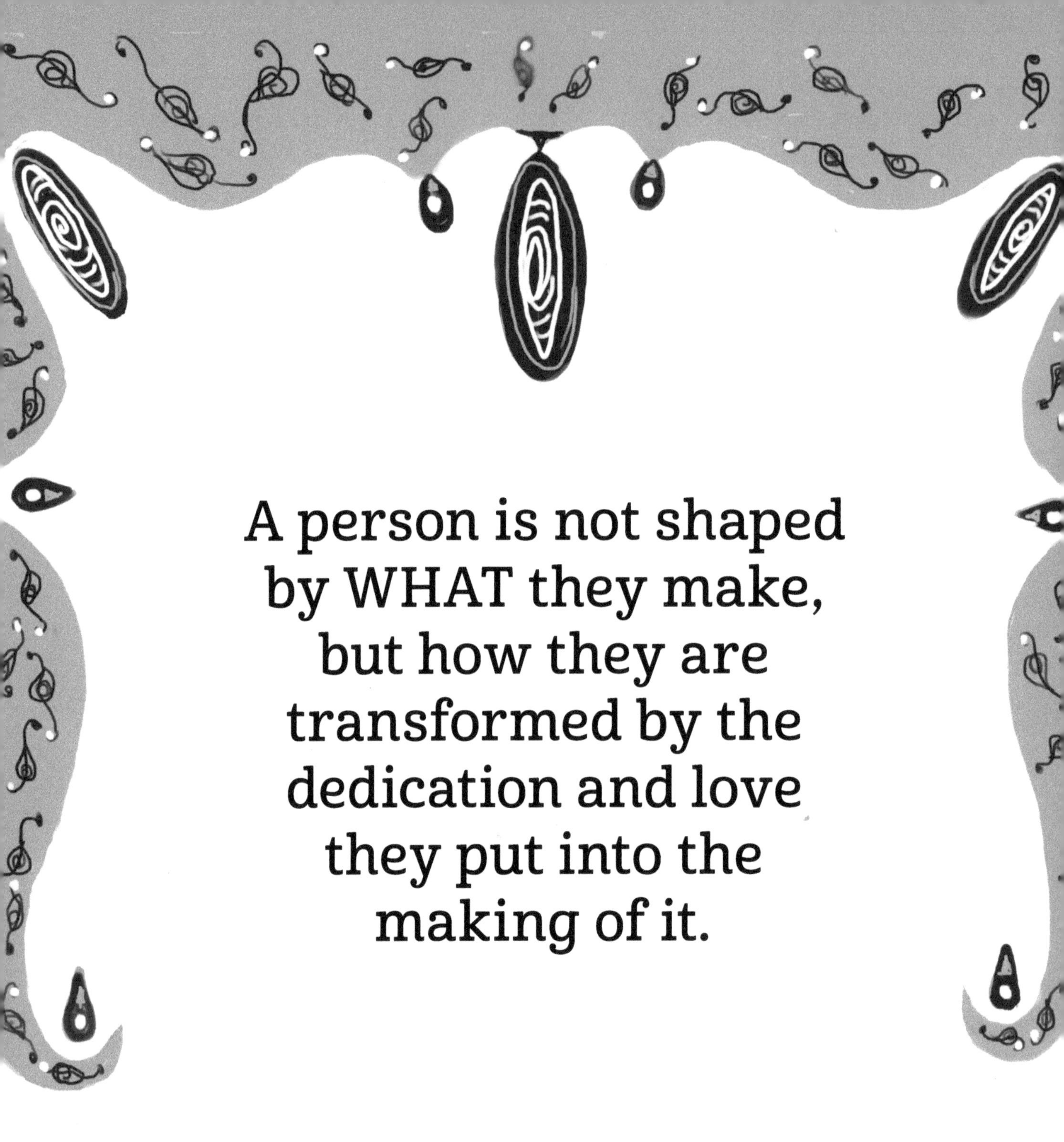
A person is not shaped
by WHAT they make,
but how they are
transformed by the
dedication and love
they put into the
making of it.

Devotion, Not Discipline

You want to make a solid structure for yourself, not force your way into a routine with a willpower ready to break yourself into submission. Force and effort never bring creative results. When creating a practice of creating, notice the words you use. Words carry powerful energies and meanings. Think about the energy contained in each of these words or phrases:

- Discipline
- Hard work
- Effort
- Struggle
- Striving
- Toil

These words have the cultural overtones of being in school. Their meanings may not provide you with the fuel you need when the going gets tough. You don't want to set up a structure where you can't keep the momentum going. You want to fill yourself with feelings of love and choice, as opposed to effort and obligation to a paradigm that doesn't have staying power. When designing your agreement to make time for creativity, fill your mind with words that honor yourself and your work such as:

- Dedication
- Devotion
- Faithfulness
- Constancy
- Wholeheartedness
- Loyalty
- Honor

Tell yourself:

"I will devote an hour to honoring my project today."

"I am dedicated to expressing myself wholeheartedly."

"I am faithful to my work."

"I will be loyal to my pre-agreements to create today."

Compare that kind of self-talk to this kind of self-talk: "I will strive to have the discipline to work hard with struggle and toil while I am in the chamber today." These kinds of words should make you mad enough to rebel and never show up to make art.

This is why you care about how you frame your time and your words. It matters to the sustainability of your creative practice and the quality of your project.

Your Way into *The Zone*

Technology for measurement of brain wave frequencies enable scientists to observe the reality of creativity—which was once a mysterious and ephemeral experience. The optimal frequency for creating is the alpha wave brain state, measured at eight to 12 Hertz (Hz). Alpha is a slightly altered state of mind, different from your normal waking state, which is the beta wave frequency, 12 to 38 Hz.

Humans can't create from the beta brain state. What they can do is critique, employ skill, edit, discern, and rationalize when in beta. To enter the powerful state of flow that creativity needs, human brains must be operating at the lower rate of the alpha frequency.

How do you go from beta to alpha? It is different for every individual. You must find your own way to *the zone* where your flow begins. Some people bring it on through a meditation practice; others use breathwork; some drink tea, or, they'll take a power nap as part of their personal plan to enter the alpha state. When you've practiced creative activity enough to set a pattern, you may be able to get into the alpha state organically. You must acclimate your body to be open to the creative state in your own way. To give you a starting point, I'll describe my own practice, and the seven-step process I provide for clients:

1. Arrive: Place your body in a safe, quiet space. Sit comfortably, with arms and legs uncrossed. Put your chin to your chest. This physical act disengages the brain.
2. Relax: Relax your belly and jaw muscles. Feel the interiors of your hands and feet.
Feel the space between your eyes.
3. Breathe: Breathe deeply to oxygenate your brain. This is a critical step that brings you to the alpha state. To better focus on your breath, close your eyes, then follow this rhythm:

- Breathe in through your nose while counting to six and imagine you are expanding

- Breathe out through your mouth while counting to six and imagine you are softening
- Breathe in this way for two to four minutes
- Then, breathe naturally

Open your eyes and be aware of the breath that is happening on its own, without you forcing it—just observe. This act brings you into the present moment—which is the key to your creativity.

4. Clearing out and releasing: Notice all your thoughts or feelings and make space for all of them by welcoming them. Don't grab on to them or run away from them. Just let them be there. Allow yourself to be exactly as you are. Continue to breathe. Now on the exhale, breathe out any feelings or thoughts that don't serve you. They are not something to get rid of. Just acknowledge them. Ask yourself if you are willing to release them on the next exhale. The exhale is where the releasing takes place. Continue to breathe and release until you have a sense of calm and peace. Extend kindness and compassion to yourself. Feel the genuineness of your intention. Be the observer of your body. Can you feel the subtle aliveness inside your entire body? Feel your blood inside your body. Feel your heartbeat. Feel the energy inside the container of your body. That is your life force.

Now feel the innocence of your soul, which wants to make something—it wants to create your *one thing* with you.

5. Enter the silence: This is the wordless, spacious, and present place of stillness inside your body. All creativity begins in a place of silence. To get there, ask yourself: "Can I feel the stillness outside and around me?" Even if there are noises in the environment, underneath is a silence. Find it and connect to it. Now ask, "Can I feel the stillness inside of me?" Even if your thoughts are on a wild ride, even if you have an ache in your back and it's demanding attention, there is a silent space inside of you. Believe in it. Connect with it in order to bring a sense of stillness to your body.

6. Expand the field: Now open your field of awareness. Broaden your attention so that you can feel far out from your body. Imagine expanding your energy and attention out into the world.

7. Enter the safe chamber in your mind and begin: If you feel spacey, that's OK. If you feel like you don't know what to do, that's OK too. Be willing to be in the state of not knowing. Sit down with your creative tools (instrument, computer, paints, canvas, pen, paper, etc.) and create.

The first time you do any of this, it might be uncomfortable. It might be too much awareness for you to handle. It's OK. Like in meditation, it's the attention you put on the experience that matters, not whether you're doing it "right." There is no right way or wrong way. Notice that when you keep adding to your awareness, your beta state slides away, and you enter the alpha brain wave patterns that allow you to be creative.

Breathe
through
the HEART to
break through
in the art.

The Six Shortcuts to Flow

After a while you'll get into your own rhythm of entering the alpha state for creating and you won't need any list to guide you into *the zone*. It will just happen when you sit down and begin. If you are having trouble focusing, the following is a quick six step reminder to help you settle down and get going again. This guidepost is helpful to me when my mind is racing, and I need a kick-start.

1. **Show up and sit down.**
2. **Slow down.** I mean, really slow down. The brain is fast. You want to move in a peanut butter kind of slow. This is slow-motion time and when your body begins to slow down, so does your brain.
3. **Still yourself.** Drop down and move your awareness away from your head. Put your attention on the inside of your pelvis. This is the way of embodiment. Rest your chin on your chest and breathe in and out, slow, easy, up to 20 times. This gives your mind's chatter time to exit and leave you to your true self.
4. **Silence.** Feel the silence around you. Pass over the actual noise—go underneath it to silence. Now find the silence inside yourself.
5. **Spread out.** Now imagine that true self that you have accessed and spread that energy out into the world. You will feel a oneness and a sense that you are a part of everything.
6. **Start.** Pick up your tools and begin.

Where Can I Relax?

Creativity at its best can only occur in a state of relaxation. If you're tense, you're in the beta brain wave state; you're looking to produce results and control the outcome. The flow state requires softening. How do you relax?

> *I am an excitable person. Relaxation was a big lesson for me. One of the best questions I ask myself is: "Where can I relax?"*
>
> *Where in my body? Where doesn't have to be a physical place—which is why I ask this question often. I set an emotional GPS scan for directions on how to soften in situations like meeting a new person, when dealing with technological challenges, preparing for sleep, while writing an email, and even during an act of lovemaking! It helps me connect and go deeper.*

When people tell you to "just relax," you often feel some form of resistance. This is natural—you've been judged. And then, you judge yourself by thinking that you wouldn't have gotten tense in the first place if you were a superior person who felt no lack or fear.

But asking yourself "Where can I relax?" is not a judgment—it is seeking a sense of possibility. It suggests to your mind that you are only searching for something. Use this question as your scanner for three areas:

Body: Places you may feel clenched (toes, knees. belly, shoulders, jaw)

Heart: Places where you feel protection, anger, gratitude, forgiveness

Head: Places where your "shoulds" keep creativity at bay

My answer to this question lets me find all kinds of places for relaxation and softening, from my head to my toes.

The whole effect is that of softening, and when you soften the harsh places, you are more receptive to flow. Catch the "should" that constricts you, find the places in your body that may be holding tension, and see where your heart is hardened.

I was preparing for a storytelling performance. My intention was to "connect" with the audience. I did the body/heart/head scan and saw there was tension in my heart area. Maybe it was from excitement, maybe it was from self-protection due to a little fear about revealing my personal aspects of the story.

So, I asked the question, "Where can I relax?" It softened me a little and with that softening, I saw that everyone out there was human, like me. The more I could be like them (as in, 'we are all in this together'), the more connected I could feel to them. With the intention of "connection," I was able to scan through the lens of that focus.

The softening of those protective mechanisms in my heart area, as well as relaxing my body, gave me the most personally satisfying performance that I could remember. I felt powerful, but also very much myself while being tuned into the audience members and their responses. I wasn't putting on a show for them, trying to "do well;" I was sharing my humanity with them. I may not have been able to get there had I not done the relaxation scan.

Afterwards, many people came up to me with their own stories that related to mine. It felt very fulfilling to me, both personally and artistically.

The Guards at the Gate

Who are the guards at your gate, and where are they when you need them? It's things like: the email ping that comes in when you're working, the friend that calls for a last-minute coffee, the password problem that drags you into a vortex of wasted time that gets past the guards, past the gate, and disrupt your flow. Right?

Well, being an artist means that you are given the opportunity to learn to have agency over your time and energy. Being your own gate and guard is a prerequisite lesson for all artists—and it is one they struggle with before they can reach mastery. The temptations are provided every day. Every day you are charged with yet another opportunity to be proactive and guard against distractions and interruptions with choices that support your productivity.

You could ask this question: "Will I let other people and distractions have their way with my sacred chamber time?" and give yourself a simple "yes" or "no" as an answer. Or, as for the best way to answer the question about gates and guards, you can just say, "I am the guard of my gate so I can do my soul's work during my chamber time today."

I imagine holding up the symbol of a stop sign and saying out loud, "NO!" The idea that the word "no" can be a complete sentence is useful. Keep it in mind when you must set up some dragons at your gate. It's ironic, but people respect you more when you say, "I'm sorry, I'm not available."

Make it non-personal. Establish a blanket policy that applies to everyone: "I'm sorry, but I've promised to say no to social events until my series is ready." Or, "I'm sorry I cannot meet you for lunch. I'm on a writing diet for the next two months." Explain your commitment to yourself by saying, "Until my deadline, I'm only available to play on Sundays."

My client, Marjorie, who is a Buddhist, imagines that dragons guard and protect her temple until she is finished with her work for the day. Guard and protect your time in the chamber like a fierce dragon that is breathing fire.

Rolling with the Pleasure

The smell of paint, the way the guitar feels in your hand, the way that pen feels as it glides across the page. The tools of creativity are often delicious and sensual. Papers and beautiful pens. Colors and textures of wools, and other fabrics. The gleam of the guitar's wooden base and its taut strings. You are meant to experience creative pleasure in your life, no matter how society wants to shame you out of it. Sometimes, just appreciating your creative tools and the way your body appreciates the act of creating is worth reveling in. The pleasure you experience continues to call you back, again and again.

> *I love calligraphy. I love the paper and the ink as I dip the nibs in and make the strokes. I'm not very good at it yet, but I love doing it. I end up with ink blobs all over the paper and my letters are seldom consistent, but I can't help it, I find it so pleasurable. I want to keep playing with calligraphy because I find it so sensual. That alone keeps me coming back for more.*

You may not play the guitar in a way that you want to yet, but there is something in you that says, "keep picking it up." Recognize that the pleasure you receive in the simple experience of hearing and strumming the chords is good enough. Will you let the Impeccable Artist keep telling you that, unless you are Stevie Ray Vaughn, playing your guitar is not a worthy use of your time? No. Keep showing up and spending time with the guitar. Enjoy its smooth surface and the sounds that you make with it. Get to know it, so you can know how you learn. Explore the music that moves your soul. When you are curious and hungry enough, you will get to the next level. Make a phone call to get some lessons or watch a YouTube tutorial. It will happen if you keep your Impeccable Artist at bay and make your relationship with this guitar your priority. Even if you play for 20 minutes a day, keep reminding yourself how good it feels to hold the instrument and feel the sounds of the strums in your body. Make the pleasure more important than your assessment of where you are in your learning.

You can bypass the circuitry of inner criticism, which art will teach you, when you lose the squeezing effects of the Impeccable Artist and if you concentrate on deserved, simple pleasure.

Tell yourself: "Based on my skill set now, I am having fun. I am learning. I'm rolling with the pleasure of making. That is enough."

Grasping for the Passion

In creativity, just as in a sustainable love relationship, after the first delirious, heart-dancing, crack-addled period of obsession, you eventually fall into a different kind of love. You don't always need to show up for date night with stars in your eyes. But in a sustainable relationship—with a lover or with your creativity—you always show up.

Once you identify as being a creative, you can't expect that you will always have the same feeling of being high on love or life that you did in the beginning. Creativity, like love, goes through phases. Sometimes, phases of neutrality and/or the feelings of blah-ness show you that something needs to change. Sometimes it tells you that you are developing a curiosity for another aspect of the work (such as learning to draw or to take dance lessons from a professional). Sometimes, these uninspired phases speak to you of a need to go deeper, to pay more attention, or, to re-stimulate yourself by seeking inspiration from a new source.

And then, something unexpected will happen. You may feel excited again—or—you may change directions entirely.

It is unrealistic to think that you will always feel passion for your project. Like a relationship, it is normal to go through phases and waves in varying levels of emotional highs and lows.

The Horrible "Hows"

As you are making, creating, and expressing, there will always be decisions to make, steps to take, and new things to learn. It's the nature of the beast. If you approach a new project with an expected clear template for the actions you must accomplish in order to have the certainty that it will all turn out, you are missing the point of the creative process. Creative projects never turn out like you think they will or should. They may turn out better, they may be a gateway project to the next one, or, they may be tossed in the trash to be recycled. All of these will be good experience on the road of learning.

Unfortunately, the life of a project has a mind of its own. You can't expect to control all the details. You must live with a modicum of uncertainty and trust that everything will be revealed, even if it all comes into being by feeling your way through the dark incrementally. The arbitrary projection you may feel while asking about the "how"s can kill a project before it ever gets started. It can feel too overwhelming.

If you can offer yourself the suspension of disbelief and know you were led to this for a reason (even a reason not known to your logical mind), then you could offer yourself a sense of adventure and believe that you will find your way, step-by-step. You may meet a detour or go down some cobbled roads and get lost, but you will be led to your next step when you get to the next intersection. Some helper will be there to guide you. You may have an insight that suggests that you had made some assumptions before, but now you see a clear next step.

The creative mindset is difficult to describe. It's as if creatives need to throw their arms open to the universe and say, "Take me. I will abide by your decisions and I will follow your guidance!"

The first step in any endeavor is to just begin. When you take the first step, the next one will appear…then the next.

Discomfort is Our Down Payment
for Creating Anything of Value

The Threshold

It's the craziest phenomenon. You've committed to your *one thing*. You have made time in your day. You may be even enthusiastic about your project, and yet…it's hard to cross the threshold of your chamber time. This is an uncomfortable experience common to all artistic souls. Know that as you suddenly need to Google flying trapeze artists or drive to the mall to try on the latest in athletic lounge wear, you are not alone.

The gap between "normal" life and "chamber" life is wide. Let yourself feel the energetic dissimilarity and discrepancy between the two. I feel an increase of anxious feelings as I enter *the zone*. The anxiety might be rooted in fear that I will not even enter the chamber! And I know in that case, I will feel bad about myself at the end of the day. Or, maybe I fear my Impeccable Artist giving me some terrible, very bad, no good advice, such as:

"You probably won't do it right."

"Why are you qualified to write a book?"

"This has already been said by people smarter than you."

Or, it can be my discomfort about facing the unknown—even though I know it is always where the work of creativity will take me. The unknown can feel like jumping off a cliff or preparing to walk across hot coals. Here are several things to know: expect it, notice it, accept it, allow it, laugh about it:

Expect it. Yes, expect discomfort as you approach the zone. Wherever, why-ever, and whatever the reason for this difficulty in crossing the threshold and beginning to create is, I have come to learn the only way to conquer it is to expect it. Here is how it sounds: "Well, here it is again, the resistance to start, even though I've made room for creating in my schedule. I may feel resistant to crossing the threshold, but today I'm going to do it anyway."

Notice it. Report on your findings to yourself. Say: "I am resistant to starting this poem. I notice I want to Google obscure things. I notice I am holding off from starting." Keep reporting your progress to yourself: "I feel time wasting, so I'm going to get off the internet and open my journal. Where is my good pen?"

Accept it. Accept and normalize by saying, "Well, here we are again. I might as well surrender to this awkward uncomfortableness. I accept these feelings in my body. I know everybody goes through this. I am not alone."

Allow it. It's best to do this by saying, "So, welcome resistance! Come on in and have a seat. I'm going to get to work anyway."

Laugh about it. When you think about it, this phenomenon is so damn crazy that you kind of need to laugh about it. I mean, think about it…the utter ridiculousness of resistance showing up regarding the thing you want to do that would make you the most fulfilled in life is plain nonsense. But there it is. It's a mystery. And it happens to all artists. Nothing to do but laugh about it and move through it.

I often have to say to myself, "This is going to feel really uncomfortable until you get in the seat." I also know, within a few minutes of sitting down, the anxiety will go away and I'll get into the flow…which is the opposite of anxiousness.

Be your own science experiment. Notice your reactions are when you are about to cross into your chamber. Ask yourself:

"How do I feel before I sit down to go into my chamber: Resistant, anxious, self-doubting, irritable, intensity, excitement, or ___________?"

"Can I locate the discomfort I'm feeling in my body? Is my stomach tight, is my throat squeezing, am I doing shallow breathing, or is my heartbeat increasing?"

"What is going on with my thoughts as I feel the discomfort?"

"How will it feel when I sit down and begin to work?"

Now, sit down and go into your chamber. Start something.

Note the differences in your feelings after you've made the leap.

The more you notice your reactions before and after you begin to work, the easier it will be to work through it in a healthy manner.

The Passage of Discomfort

Every single day when I sit down to write, I expect to feel discomfort while crossing the threshold of ordinary life into *the zone*. On the days that I do not work on my art, I must admit to myself that I did not or could not or was not willing to pass over the threshold, and I feel bad about myself. My excuses, my ego, won that day.

So, I've learned that there is never a day when I cannot show up. I must create, even if for 15 to 30 minutes. What I have found to be empowering is knowing that the discomfort of crossing the threshold lasts only a few minutes. I've shared this knowledge with my clients who've benefited from it, too.

Crossing this threshold can be compared to what it's like when an introvert goes to a party. She knows she will endure the first awkward moments of saying hello, meeting strangers, and getting her hands on a glass of wine, until she acclimates and gets into the flow/fun of the party.

Introvert or extrovert—does anyone ever really want to go to the gym? Does anyone really want to drag themselves out of bed and put on those damn stinky shoes? Even in the first five minutes of working out, I feel like I am slogging my way along until my endorphins kick in and the movement starts to feel good. In extreme cases, like the nerves that rush through me right before I give a speech, crossing any threshold takes a powerful willingness to endure those damn nerves. Expecting it, I can see the warrior's or hero's journey inherent in the willingness to endure the discomfort. Knowing it will not last long, I can go through it with a little more ease and willingness.

Those examples are similar to the discomfort people feel when facing the act of preparing to create. There is a transition from discomfort—going from resistance to flow—that usually lasts five minutes. Then, there is the empowerment I feel once I have crossed to the other side. Knowing about, and expecting, the discomfort is what gets me into the flow.

Treacherous Moments Before You Leap

Before you begin a session in your creative chamber, be prepared to fight off absolutely anything that wants to divert your attention. You may develop cravings to obtain chocolate covered peanuts, a sudden need to Google hotels in Italy, or, taking your car for a wash might look like a good time. These voices of obstruction and antagonism are working on you in their sneaky ways. They are tricksters who want to rob you of your light.

Here's my own story while writing this book:

> *In the early days I would tell myself, "I'm going to write today." And then the regular routines and obligations of life got in the way, or my friends and family would get in the way, or... well, I would get in the way. At the end of each day I felt hollow and berated myself for lacking in fortitude.*
>
> *"How's your book coming?" my people asked.*
>
> *"Oh, it's coming," I muttered, feeling like a fraud.*
>
> *Finally, utterly miserable with myself, I took to making a daily two-hour slot for writing and commanded myself to get in the chair with no negotiation.*
>
> *I noticed in the minutes before I sat down, I would get anxious, edgy, and my brain raced. I might suddenly be gripped by the urge to Google the mating habits of polar bears, to clean out my sock drawer, or call a friend to "check in."*
>
> *I came to think of these unhealthy urges as my ego's need to keep things safe and normal, not growing, not doing the thing that is ultimately fulfilling to my life.*
>
> *It's so much easier to do things you have certainty about. Things you know how to do rather than face the scary chair with the looming blank screen mired with uncertainty. What if I don't say it right, what if I'm laughed at, what if I wasn't saying anything unique, what if it wasn't*

good enough? What if I WASN'T GOOD ENOUGH? What makes me think I'm a writer? Who did I think I was, anyway?

The more I noticed this phenomenon as I determinedly began to regularly sit down in the chair, the more I started to laugh. I began to see these insane urges as a bunch of soldiers desperately trying to obstruct me from fulfilling my dreams. Offering up anything; any dumb thing they could think of! They loved trying to send me down rabbit holes of time suckers, like taking inane personality quizzes online.

I began to expect them, to welcome them daily.

"Oh, here you are again trying to stop me. Well, today you aren't going to win. Buckle up there in the back seat. You can't touch the dials, you can't touch the wheel, cuz I'm driving today."

Other days, it was a bigger battle, and I was required to use a more forceful approach.

"Shut the @#$%, up! I'm writing now."

I notice it always takes up to 10 minutes after I get in the driver's seat until those voices fall asleep like a cranky toddler, head lobbing about, strapped in the car seat. My edgy anxiety drifts away.

Once I was zoning, I was engaged again, and I was in a safe territory where I could not hear their nonsense, or the noise would stop altogether. So, for that day, I prevailed!

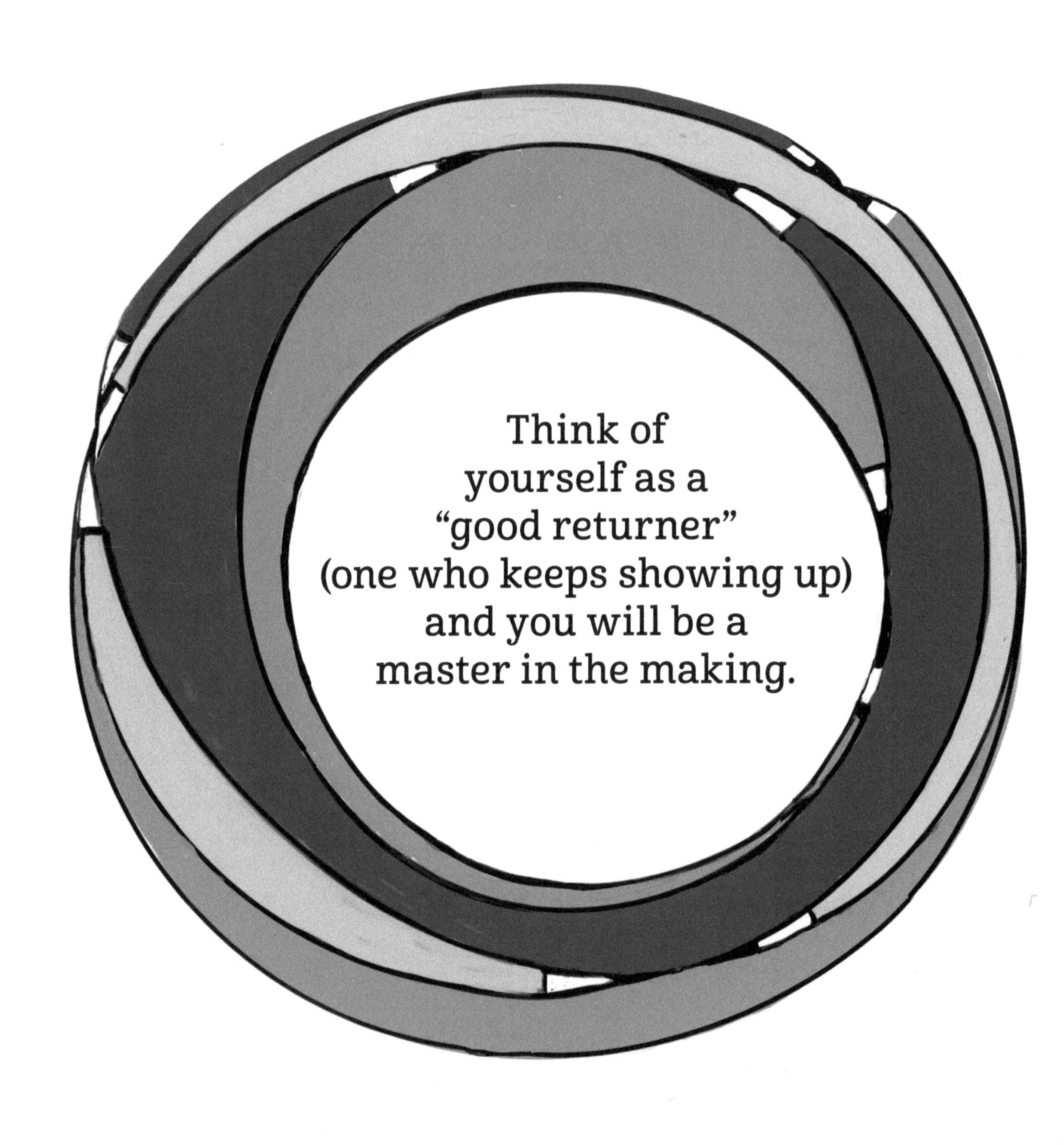
Think of
yourself as a
“good returner”
(one who keeps showing up)
and you will be a
master in the making.

The Art of Returning

In creativity, my definition of the word 'mastery' is "the art of returning and beginning again." Notice this definition does not include the words 'high degree of competence,' because you develop that when you learn to master the returning. It seems the requisite condition of living a sustainable creative life is the willingness and humility to start again. And, to begin anew each day.

The key to returning on your path towards mastery is practicing withstanding the discomfort of crossing the threshold. Carve out an amount of time, no matter what your terrible, no good, very bad voices say:

"I don't know what to do next."

"I don't want to ruin it."

"The conditions today aren't right—and—the conditions have to be right."

"I think it's shit. I don't want to waste time on shit."

"I don't feel like it. I should feel like it."

"I'm in a bad mood."

"I'll do it tomorrow."

Think of yourself as a "good returner," one who keeps showing up, and you will be a master in the making.

Once you
begin trusting
yourself, your
creativity
grows in
abundance.

Creative Confidence

Every single time you push yourself out of your comfort zone, you manufacture more confidence. Confidence feels good, even in small increments. Learning a new skill, trying a new style of painting, telling the truth, having a difficult conversation, taking a class in pottery—doing anything that pushes you beyond your identity of self and routines.

Every time more confidence drops in, you grow new neurons in your brain, and you get a shot of dopamine. Confidence creates energy in your body. It is a physical experience. Your energetic vibration expands as you reach for more experiences in which to test yourself. This is the cycle of action and reward. You may hear yourself say, "Hey. That worked. I can do this. I am proud of myself. I want more."

The confidence you gain causes you to trust yourself as you expect the discomfort as a sign that you are about to step through a doorway that ultimately feels like a reward.

The muses love you when you dare to face the unknowns. They reward your willingness with even more connection to them. Surprising, happy accidents occur that make your work more unique. Each incident you experience where source was listened to, when you acted on impulse, further strengthens your confidence in yourself and your connectivity to that great big beautiful source of possibility.

It's a cycle, this building of confidence. Not a vicious cycle. It's a delicious one.

Leave a Trail of Breadcrumbs

It's challenging to come back to your creative work. The threshold beckons, but is hard to cross every day, especially when you have been away in your regular life for a while. Being on a vacation, or living through the holidays, can have a way with your schedule. Under the best of circumstances getting back into creative momentum is a challenge but starting back after having been away is particularly difficult. There is always the voice of the Impeccable Artist and the fear voice of the ego to ignore. Then there are the people in your life who offer up constant needs for attention. Oh, and what about your to do lists with their own voices that call out, "Tend to me first!"

It's a wonder any of us get anything done.

But I can offer two ideas that support you to do your *one thing* that will ultimately support your dreams:

Leave a trail of breadcrumbs for the next day. Stop your work in an area that lights you up, an area you are just beginning to explore and find interesting. Leave it for the day so you will look forward to getting back to it the next day. This has the added benefit of letting your subconscious, your Guidance, do some work overnight. You will arrive the next day ready to explore and possibly create with a new perspective.

Have an intention to finish something specific and concrete. Do this by telling yourself: "Today, I will finish painting the sky." "Today, I will edit three chapters." "Today, I want to complete the bridge in the song." "Today, I will send the poem to a literary journal editor."

This will make it easier to cross the threshold because you've got your inner GPS set to something specific. Once you are in *the zone*, anything can happen, but setting a small intention will give your brain a constructive job. Brains in any wave state like to have jobs!

Break It Down

When you are stuck, counterintuitively, persistence is not always your best friend. Persistence has a role, but when it comes to creative solutions, dogged persistence can backfire. When you're thinking about a problem, the more time you spend deliberating, the more your focus narrows. You lose sight of the big picture and become fixated on the details. At this point you have reached a point of diminishing returns on your efforts.

What do you do? Put your attention elsewhere. Focus on another project for a while and come back to it when you can see it with fresh eyes. Move your body, take a walk, make a cup of tea. "Eureka!" moments often come when you have your attention outside yourself and the problem.

Scheduling shorter, more frequent sessions helps you, too. By planning multiple periods of deep thinking, along with periods of re-focus, you're guaranteeing that your focus expands.

If you're having resistance in taking the next step, break it down. Cut the step-in half. Then cut each next step in half. Make it as small and slow as you can.

Obstacles

In every creative life, obstacles will show up. What do these obstacles look like? Not knowing the next right step, not having enough skill in a certain area, working with new materials, using new technology, not creating enough time, not having enough energy, or even a failure to fund your project.

When you are working in the state of flow in your life and work, obstacles are a means to an end. The Impeccable Artist will get frustrated, stressed, and make you feel a sense of lack. From the Impeccable Artist's point of view, obstacles should be considered stop signs. The Impeccable Artist will have you believe that something from the outside, or your own incompetence, is thwarting you. Instead, obstacles are often opportunities to expand, they may signal a next step is presenting itself. When you stay within the flow state, your pure creative state, you will see that obstacles are like steppingstones to areas of growth. Seeing, and overcoming obstacles strengthens the foundation of your project. Obstacles can be overcome more easily in this state of flow, where you maintain your relationship to your project's greater intelligence.

Phases of the Game: The Next Level Up

If you've hit a wall, you may just be in a new phase.

"This is just a mess."

"I don't know what to do."

"I have no idea what I'm doing."

"I'm out of my league here."

Think of the creative process as a video game. Each time you complete one level, you are required to learn new skills and best practices of the next level up. In creativity, there are no signs that say, "Congratulations, Ninja! you are now moving to the Warrior 12 level!" All you know is you have hit a challenge and you've got to learn something new in order to keep going. Thinking of it as a ninja warrior who is gathering new tools and skills for the next step is a more empowering mental construct than, "I'm stuck."

This new level requires you to learn new skills, establish new work habits, create new beliefs, or to figure out a new way of looking at your project. The next level may require you to give up old ways of doing something and develop a new way. The next level up may mean you have to ask someone for help, or, find new resources. These are the many levels/challenges on the road to mastery, the next level of the hero's journey.

At one point while writing this book, I realized I had way too many chapters. I became completely overwhelmed and was verbally beating myself up in frustration. Then I realized I had just reached a new level. "Time for organization," I said to myself. "I'm good at that. Now I just have to do it with the book."

My client Cathy went from learning to knit, to making clothing, to selling it in shops, to creating an online platform for her knitting brand. When we thought of each step as though it was a challenging video game, every encounter with the unknown was more manageable for her. And there were steep learning curves along the way, especially as she wrestled with technology.

What are your challenges? Do you see the levels your project will allow you to reach?

Benefits of Time Restrictions

When time is limited and you are frustrated, it can be an enhancement instead of a struggle. I was just beginning a new oil painting and the canvas was huge. I knew I only had 45 minutes but was eager to begin. I told myself that my only job was to fill the canvas with paint. I could change the rest later, but at the end of those 45 minutes I wanted to have completely laid down the first layer. With that intention in mind: "just start by filling the canvas," I stopped thinking, analyzing, and fighting time. At the end of those 45 minutes, I was delighted with the freshness and instinctual quality of the painting. I had used limited time with intentionality to great result.

You may also need to give up telling this story: "I can only be creative if I have unlimited time to get into *the zone*. If I can't have four hours, then I can't write/paint/practice." What if you only have two hours or even 30 minutes? You can make a choice instead of being a victim to your schedule. Ask yourself, "What may I do today, given I have only two hours? What shall I focus on?"

Link your desire and the vision to those two hours. You may find you are even more productive in a smaller container of time, especially if you connect to the way you want to feel at the end of the session. Many books have been written on the practice of creativity for only 15 to 30 minutes a day. There is a lot of wisdom about this method.

I had to give up control of the outside circumstances of my life and rejigger my perspective when my mom fell and fractured her hip. After caring for her, there was little left in my day to create. I could not control those circumstances, but I could create small incremental uses of my time, even if it was making an idea list or writing for 15 minutes.

Even the space of 15 minutes produces momentum forward. It is a fallacy to think that the only time to create is when you have the freedom of a half a day to spend. If you only have a 15-minute slot of time, just know that your subconscious will be working on it while you are away from the project. You are still making headway.

The Art of the Start

Sometimes it is just the starting that is the hardest. The long approach to the threshold feels like too much work. You see the mess that is the project, (whether it's an ongoing one or one you haven't yet begun) and you realize it's going to be too much trouble to get going and feel satisfied. The whole thing is a foolhardy mission and you wish you'd never set yourself up for failure. You are embarrassed you ever mentioned your *one thing* to anyone. You want to burn the evidence in your journal—that page where you came up with your *one thing*.

This is normal. It's a common derailment caused by the voices of obstruction.

Observe those "about to cross the threshold" fears and anxieties and notice that as soon as you sit down to begin, they will recede. I am getting a kick out of mine these days. The voices now sound humorous:

"It's too much trouble today."

"I don't know how to begin."

"This is a confusing place in the book."

"By the time I lay out my paints it'll be time to stop."

"I should go to the dry cleaners first."

When I observe them from a distance, knowing that the anxiety will be over as soon as (or shortly after) I cross the damn threshold of the chamber, I can be jolly about them. They're only temporary visitors. The other benefit is that every time I let the voices diminish their power over me, I gain confidence and a sense of agency over my life.

It also helps to have an intention for the next step you plan to take when you again cross the threshold. Making small plans as you cross the anxiety-ridden threshold will shore you up. Hear yourself say:

"Today I will just do the background of the painting."

"Today I will memorize 1 page of my script."

"Today I'm going to take a look at what I wrote yesterday to see if it has a logical storyline."

"Today I will sculpt in the yard, to see the material better under natural light."

Remember, you're wanting to be feeling the flow, so plan for it. Then expect the unexpected and greet it with a sense of wonder.

And, on the topic of sense, it's important to have a sense of humor about how annoying the start of a project can be. I imagine that a parachutist who is about to jump out of an airplane has accepted the panic beforehand. You are not a parachutist. You are a creative—just jumping into making art. While it may pale in comparison to skydiving, the voices of resistance can be just as terrible. A sense of humor will smooth the way to your start.

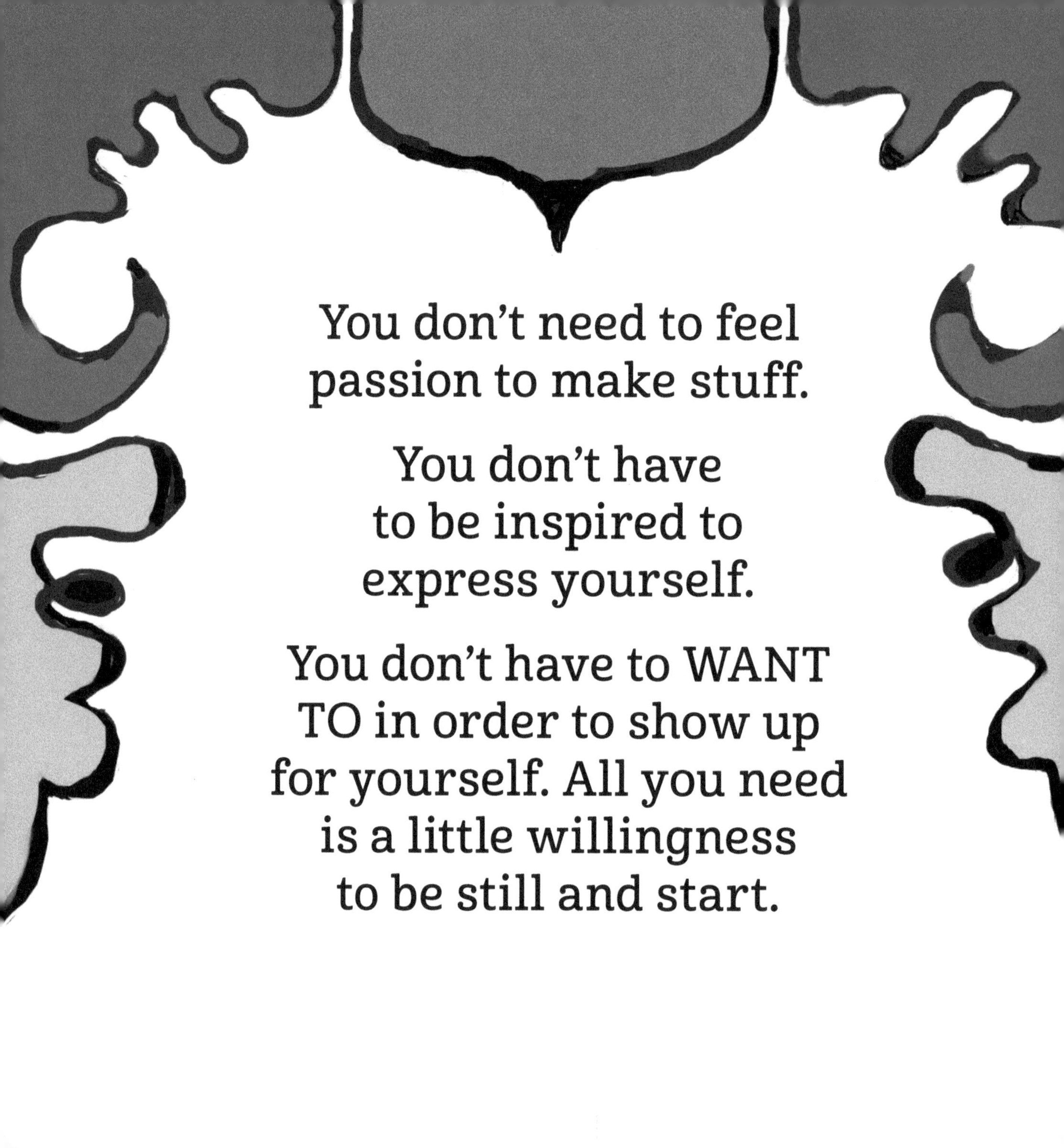

You don't need to feel passion to make stuff.

You don't have to be inspired to express yourself.

You don't have to WANT TO in order to show up for yourself. All you need is a little willingness to be still and start.

Anti-Postponement Strategies

When you find you are postponing your work for the day, here are some strategies to get you going again.

The Blast-off: Make your move into the discomfort zone of starting. Count from one to five and then, in the courage moment, say, "GO!" The counting gives you a chance to regroup and choose to be brave in the face of discomfort. "1, 2, 3, 4, 5…GO!"

Count Time in Micro-units: Work in small increments of time. Instead of thinking of tasks in long-range terms, use up a five- to 10-minute period for doing what you want, refusing to not put off anything that brings you satisfaction. I often say to myself, "I can do anything for five minutes." This is also helpful when you feel antsy and want to quit before you are satisfied with your work for the day. "I will work 10 minutes more. I can do anything for 10 minutes."

The Worst Thing Question: "What is the worst thing that could happen to me if I did what I'm putting off right now?" The answer revealed is usually so ridiculous or insignificant that it may help you break through. Assess your fear and you'll have no reason to hang onto it. "If I wrote this chapter and it was hard and I couldn't find the right words, I would…"

"…get frustrated and feel really bad about myself."

"…feel terrible and quit the damn thing entirely!"

Asking this question and hearing the answer often produces ideas that will kick-start you into some reasonable action. For instance, one day I felt lost while writing this book and decided to work on the easy stuff. I thought I'd save writing the important ideas for another day. At least the question got me moving again; writing the small ideas.

The Worthy One: Think of yourself as too significant to live with anxiety about the things you must do. Remind yourself of your worth and remember that people who feel worthy are not victims of their own goals. People who honor themselves and their visions for their lives don't turn away from themselves.

The Doing: Remind yourself that it's the doing that matters, not your false ideas of perfection. One act of courage can eliminate all that fear. Stop telling yourself that you must perform well. Remind yourself that doing it is far more important.

The Payoff Question: What are the payoffs for delaying that which will ultimately fulfill you? Possible answers (and they're not good answers, by the way):

"I get to hold on to my identity as the giver; as someone who never got to produce my art because I wanted to be known as an unselfish person."

"If I don't try, I'll never have to fail. Or worse, win."

"My ex would be right—she always said I wasn't creative."

The Do-or-Die Question: Are you doing what you'd choose to be doing if you knew you had six months to live?

If you want your life to change for the better, don't complain about it. Do something. Rather than wasting your time and energy with immobilizing anxiety over what you are putting off, just take one step right now. The anxiety will fade once you do.

Be a doer, not a wisher.

The Best Creativity Hack

1. ARRIVE in your creative space.
2. DO one small thing.

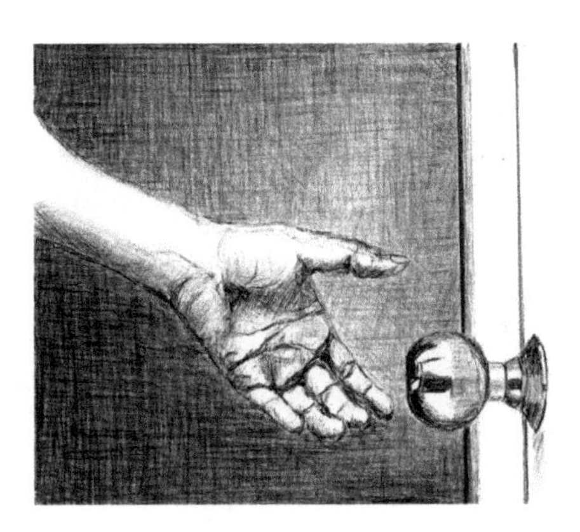

Doodling is
not SERIOUS,
but it is
IMPORTANT.

When you’re not clouding
your head with judgment
and critique, there is fresh
energy to create anew.

The Doodle Zone

I believe in doodling. I've doodled in the margins of every notebook I used for each class I ever took. I doodle in my journal, and I doodle for a few minutes before I start to write on a project.

Here is a note Deborah, my so-called "creatively stuck client," sent me after she had begun doodle-journal writing for a week:

> *"Everything slows down. My brain stops spinning with how much there is to do. All the frustration and overwhelm is dissipating. I go to a wordless place and can listen better to inspiration. Inspiration and ideas start to flow into me and out through the pen. Inspiration comes in where there is no trying, pushing, forcing or begging. The ideas aren't coming from what I think I should say in order to be "successful," or something someone else would like. They are coming from me and what I like. When I'm doodling, anything is possible, everything is fun.*
>
> *"It makes me present. I can listen. I can fly. I get ideas. I can doodle around the ideas. It's not about the results, it's about the place it takes me. I know that we are not curing cancer here or solving world peace or winning a noble prize.*
>
> *"This is not serious, but it is important."*

So many great designs, poems, songs, dances, and stories come about when you're goofing around, playing, and just enjoying making. Feeling your fingers doing something without a plan. Playing with forms and repeating patterns. Toggling back and forth between inspiration and discernment. Asking:

"What could I make of this?"

"What would happen if I repeat that somewhere else?"

"How is this like that?"

"What does this remind me of?"

"Is there a pattern here?"

...and then, sometimes you say, "Violà, I've got something here!"

A surprise. Something new and unique that came from your inspiration, not your critical mind. Even if you didn't get something useable in the "doodle zone" you had fun and explored. You primed the pump for your work. You got out of your head. When that happens, you are living in the moment.

The reason doodling is a vital exercise for any artistic venture is because it produces positivity and reinforces the idea that your true creative potential thrives in an atmosphere of non-judgement. While doodling, you bypass the circuitry of criticism.

Doodling is also an excellent way to prepare for a period of creative work. Try it for a few minutes before you begin to work for the day. It will slow you down, get you in *the zone* and make you feel happy.

Doodling is an experience of being totally engaged in a task or activity yet completely detached from the result. There are no accidents in doodling, and you can't do it wrong. Nobody is going to grade you. There is an inverse relationship to your level of judgement and your level of creation. If you're not clouding your head with the lower vibrational energies of judgement, analysis, critique (in the beta state), there is more energy and clarity to create (in the alpha state). You cannot create and critique at the same time.

When you are without judgement, you don't waste energy seeing things from only a right or wrong perspective. When you no longer focus on finding the 'right' answer, you can instead create powerful solutions.

If you're looking for the right answer, you're using black and white thinking. When this happens, you're usually worried about making mistakes; you're concerned that your answer may turn out to be 'wrong,' particularly in the eyes of other people. Yet from a wider perspective, the reality is that for nearly all challenges, there isn't only one solution.

By learning to be totally engaged in whatever it is you do, intellectually and emotionally, and by remaining objective and detached from judgment as well as result, you will unlock your true creativity.

This is how you find happy accidents. This is where you find unique styles that have never been done before. This is how you get out of those old processes you have done before and keep repeating because they have worked in the past but now seem flat and uninteresting. This is where you start exploring again.

Play the Doodle Zone game: Squiggle some kind of shape onto a paper with a pen. See if you can expand it, enhance it, make it into something pleasing. Move your tools around with no story. Just move. See what happens when you are not trying to please anyone but yourself. You're just playing, looking to please yourself. See if you can find design in it. See if you can find patterns. See the colors or rhythms and reinforce them. Repeat the themes. See some possible patterns emerge. Repeat the patterns.

Doodling inspires you to adopt the best attitude for creative discovery. Remember the note from Deborah: "This is not serious, but it is important."

Happy Accidents

It just happened naturally for me. Doodling started out as curiosity and a form of relaxation, and then it turned into something I put out in the world. It was a happy accident.

Doodling helps me to relax. I can get out of my head and into my heart. I feel peaceful. While looking for patterns and seeking to expand them, I stop thinking. If my mind has been busy all day, spending some time doodling grounds me. I use an iPad and an iPad pencil to play with an app known as Procreate®. It lets me make designs and add my quotes in them to use it for memes on social media.

The other benefit of doodling is that I've learned about the path of happy accidents in creativity. I created some surprising art when I thought I'd made a mistake but kept going. I was so encouraged by the result, it led me to deliberately scribble out an unconscious doodle and then play at making it pleasing to the eye. This is new art, and it comes from goofing around.

Happy accidents, I have come to believe, are the muses' way of saying "Don't take yourself too seriously." Out of chaos, you can make beauty and order, and create harmony. Happy accidents serve as reminders that getting out of your head leads to new forms, new directions, and originality.

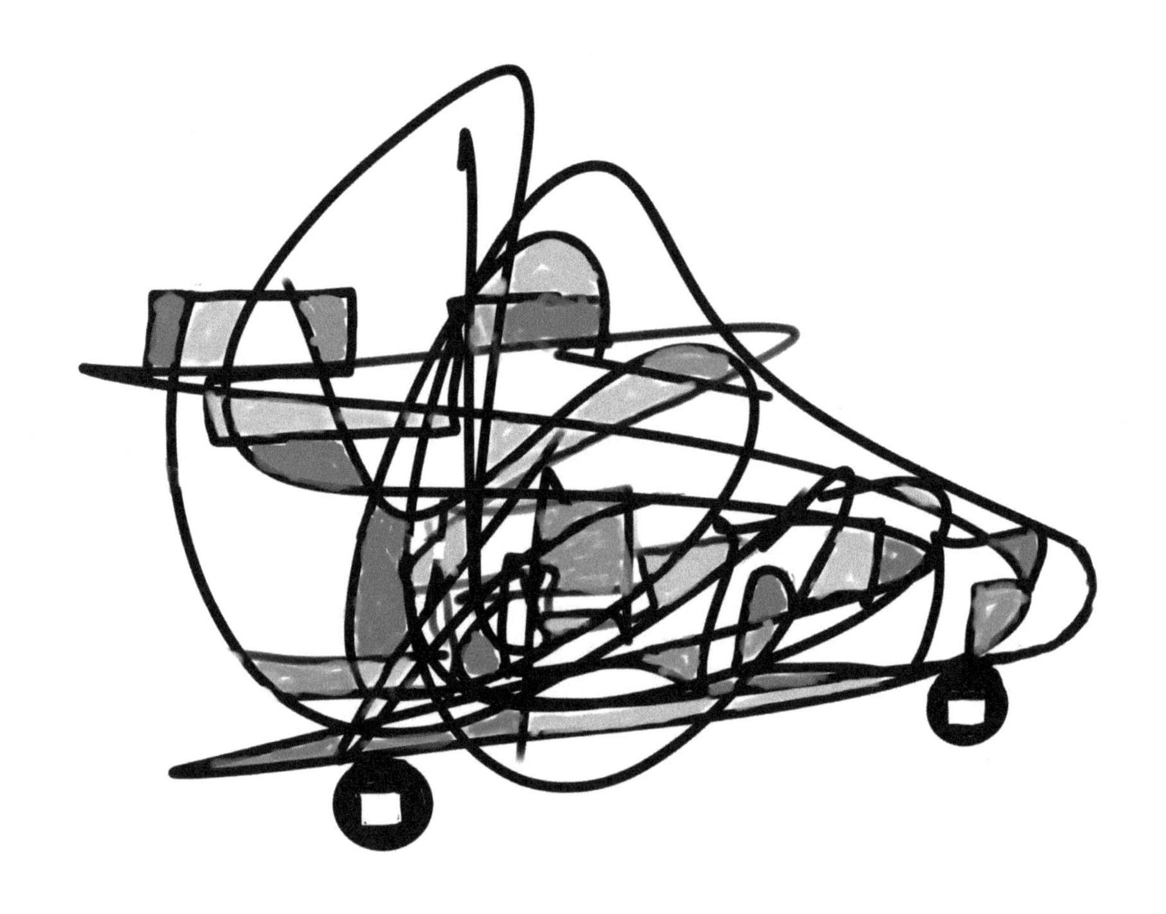

Make enough mistakes
and what have you got?
Innovation.

Lost Momentum

Have you gone away on vacation or have you suffered through a family crisis only to return to your *one thing* project and discover that the two of you had become strangers? Maybe it was that regular life got overwhelming for a long period, and when your to-do list finally settled down you couldn't locate the pertinent strands of inspiration for your project again.

When I've been away from a project, I feel like I've lost a thread and can't remember where I was or what was driving me. The longer this feeling goes on, I start to feel bad about myself. That bitch, my Impeccable Artist says things like:

"You are a dilettante."

"If you were a real artist you would be committed and be able to work anywhere."

I have to shut her down, because I know several ways to approach lost momentum.

Expect a re-discovery period. Set up the appointment with yourself to make the chamber time and show up, expecting only to reconnect. Like a spouse who has just come home from an extended trip, you sit together and talk. You "catch up" with each other. It may take a session or two, but you will fall back into the rhythm of your *one thing* again.

Know that you will come back to your *one thing* with different lenses. New perspective is a good thing. Artists know that their subconscious minds have been working even when they are absent from their projects. Who you are after time away may give a deeper perspective to your work. Know this and let the absence work for you.

"Masters of the Universe" people would have you believe that you are in sabotage mode if you lose momentum by taking a day off. Bull pucky. Sometimes you need to do something else to reset yourself. If you do it with completely no guilt, you will not have a guilty, "expectation hangover" and will come back to the project with a renewed vigor. Your subconscious will be working on your behalf while you are cleaning your closet, having a binge-worthy day, or, taking a well-deserved vacation.

The No-Story Game

Some meditators who wish to experience an empty mind help themselves focus by saying, "Thinking." This word reminds them to keep going towards the empty state. In my case, the reminder phrase is "Over-thinking." That sounds judgmental and non-spiritual, but, it's true. I'm an over-thinker.

In order to get myself out of the way as I contemplate my creative work projects, I like to say, "No story" when I'm making my doubts more important than the sitting down. Those self-doubt gremlins may be there, but I know they are just a learned response to protect myself. These habits of the mind have developed over the years, so I won't make a fool of myself, fail, or do some other awful thing. They keep me small, however, and don't allow the big place of inspiration to come, which feels open and flowy. These story voices feel constrictive and small, tight and cramped. By gently acknowledging them as being there, I also ask them to get out of the way so I can be available to something bigger that is wanting to come through.

It feels good to be simply a body walking to the kitchen to get a cup of coffee in order to go sit down and do the pre-agreed upon writing. When the bargaining comes up and sounds like, "I don't need to do it now, I could do it later. I don't feel like it today, I really should do laundry." I say, "No story," like the cool and calm mom who simply says, "garbage," or "bed" to her kids.

One word can quiet down the bargaining bitch in your mind. You are now simply a body moving to the kitchen to get coffee in order to write.

Whenever you catch yourself coming up with a grab-bag of excuses or you've got the Impeccable Artist yammering in your ear, try the "No Story" game and head off to the chamber.

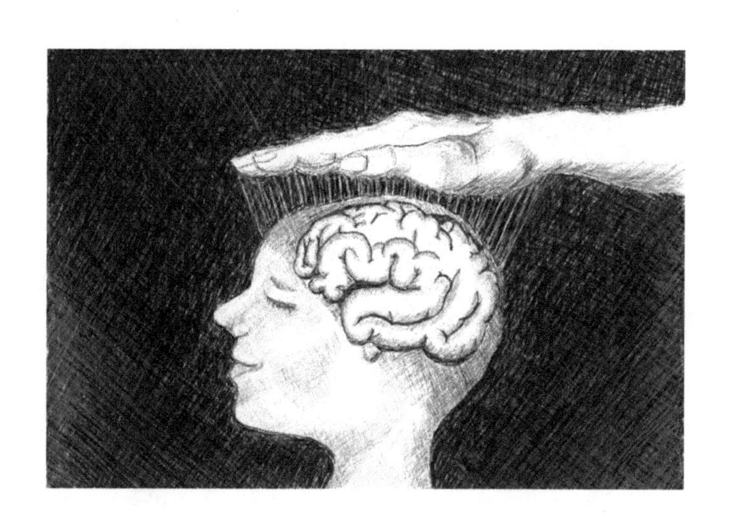

IDEAS are like red balloons
dropping from the sky.
Be glad and welcome
them (whether you decide
to use them or not).

A good balloon loves
a playful child.

Red Balloons

In an environment of no judgement, you will see the abundance of the universe and ideas will be allowed to come down with ease. Once you set an intention and open yourself to the flow of inspiration, you'll get ideas. I like to think of the ideas coming in the form of red balloons dropping down. Call it the subconscious offering solutions to your problems, call it your muses working on your behalf. It doesn't matter how you source it in your belief system. What matters is you develop a sense of trust in them and listen to them. These ideas may come to nothing that you want to explore or express in the real world, or they may be offering you ways to think outside a box you might be stuck on. They may be offering you something to explore or not. The importance is that you notice and thank the source of them. (Hey, you're not the only one who needs appreciation in order to thrive.)

Sometimes the red balloons drop down so fast you'll have to stop what you're doing just to keep up. (This is why you must always have a small notebook or journal with you.) Sometimes they will come in a dream. Most times they will drop down when you have your mind on something else, when your attention is off the problem or challenge at hand, during a bath, on a bike ride, or a walk in nature. These are times when you are living in the moment, and you drop into the alpha brain state. That's how creativity works; you relax enough, and you'll get some answers. It's a mystery and it's magic.

Let them drop all the balloons they want, I say! Just have a notebook in hand, for some will be perfect for what you're working on and some will work for what you'll be working on in the future and some will just be…balloons.

Know that receiving red balloons is just more evidence that your superconscious, your muses, your field of awareness is alive and working for you. Trust it. The more you trust, the more you get. Greet them all with pleasure and gratefulness. Meet them with a playful welcoming.

Curating Your Attention

Without waxing poetic on the evils of social media and how it is turning us all into addicts, I would like to offer a perspective about your attention. Think about the way it is given, both internally and externally. It matters to creativity that you are not a slave to distraction and diversion. It matters big time.

OK, so we all do it. We waste time on social media, texts, emails, Google and YouTube. It sucks up time and energy. There is always something or someone begging for your time, energy, and attention—and these are your most treasured resources. You've seen and responded to:

"Click Here!"

"Watch This!"

"Urgent! Response Needed Now!"

It's exhausting. It's not going away. It's getting worse by the moment. Instead of us all becoming luddites, it's going to require us bringing awareness to how it's affecting our lives. Will you let yourself become a victim to it? The key is noticing and bringing the why of it into the light so the consumption of social media can be at your own choice.

Instagram. Facebook. Twitter. Ask yourself:

"Am I seeking a distraction so that I can veg out?"

"Am I bored? Discouraged?"

"Am I looking for a meme that will inspire me or make me happy?"

"Am I using Instagram and Facebook to feel like I am keeping up with people and events so that I feel interested, interesting and important?"

There is no judgement. Just notice. That way, when you are standing in a line and you decide to check in to social media, you understand your motives. Maybe you'll say, "This is going to be a long wait. I am going to amuse myself with Instagram." Or, you could put your phone away while you are in line and tell yourself stories in your mind about the people around you. You could squint your eyes and search for designs in the room that inspire you. You could take pictures in your mind to remember and draw later.

As for emails and texts, they are indeed important tools of communication. But, notice how much time you spend returning texts and emails. Do you feel like you're accomplishing something important that will make you feel validated? Do you end the day by wondering what you did that mattered to you by attending to the outside with the obligations and distractions of other people's agendas? Are you looking for distraction to feel important or valuable to others? Is all this outside attending to other people's needs eating up your time and energy to the detriment of your important projects? Could you create a 30-minute block of time devoted to returning emails during the day after your fulfilling projects are completed?

Try this three-part thought experiment. There's a question to consider, and a list to make. Here's its first part: If you were to fully engage (with your head) in paying attention to your exterior world and its perceived obligations and distractions for two hours, how will you feel at the end?

Here is my list of feelings:

- Empty
- Constricted
- Used
- Hollow

Now for part two: If you were to fully engage in paying attention (with your heart) for two hours to your interior world and your *one thing*, how will you feel when those two hours end?

These words are on my list:

- Relieved
- Relaxed
- Recharged

- Used-up for good
- At a choice point
- Rewarded
- Fulfilled
- Satisfied

Now, the third part. How do you feel when you pay attention with your heart first, before you pay attention with your head to your exterior world?

This is how I feel:

- Like I set boundaries well
- Like I have freedom of choice

Easy

While it is true that anything worth doing is going to require dedication and effort, it is also true that creativity doesn't live in the universe of "work is supposed to be hard" and "you are supposed to suffer and struggle."

In working with your *one thing* project, especially when you are working on a deadline, there will be times when you feel stretched thin or overwhelmed. You may not know the next step to take or how to proceed. You may have boxed yourself into a corner with your characters or design. You may be feeling stressed and want to give it up. This will make you lose momentum and heart. When I am in this state, it's usually because I'm over-complicating something.

I could also be unconsciously operating in the "work is hard camp" and saying, "I should try much harder," which is why I can't see that there might be a pathway of simplicity or ease.

Another question I love and use often in my work is this one:

"What would this look like if it were easy?"

The answer for this question will put your brain on a search for simplicity. It reframes the question and lets you paint with easier and simpler strokes. You'll sing with more relaxation and dance with more fluidity.

The Paradox of Time

When you feel the presence and spaciousness of creating, you will lose yourself in the doing, and you develop a new relationship with time. For those in creation mode, time is more about the space of doing, rather than the measurement of minutes and hours. When you're in a state of doing, you may lose track of time. Time seems to have expanded. Or, maybe it contracted! You've heard the phrase, "Time is an illusion," but you may not understand what it feels like for you yet. You may know of artists or people who were 100 percent engaged in their work who've said, "...and the next thing I knew, it was 2 o'clock in the morning!"

I like to think about falling into a sinkhole of time...a magical realm where anything can happen, and I will come back to the real world having transformed into something better than my old self. But that's just me looking for pleasurable ways to want to return to the fold again and again.

The paradox about falling into this sinkhole is that once you make time for your projects with a sense of honor and dignity, your sense of time will expand once you drop into *the zone*. In order to capture time, you must claim it as your own. When you do, time will slow down...because it is really expanding into the space you're making in which to be creative.

You can make time expand even if you only have an hour in a space where your logical mind can't imagine that you'll get anything done. Enter your space with full presence and a lack of distraction, then free fall into timelessness. It's what happens when you work in the creative zone state.

Losing track of time is a clear signal that your brain has slipped from the beta—logical brain state—to either the alpha or theta brain states of creativity, inspiration, and relaxation.

Don't be surprised if you find yourself relaxed and having such a sense of enjoyment, you want to continue working on your *one thing* while ignoring the menial tasks your logical mind insists need to be done today. Beware! Remember—you cannot create and critique at the same time! Let yourself develop a new relationship to your creativity and your obligations. There is something about creating in *the zone* that rolls itself into allowing you to re-jigger the things on your list that are "priorities." Creatives who practice their art often get creative-er even in the ways they make time to pay bills, feed the dog, and take out the trash!

What if today was simple?
What hardness inside
could I *UN-CLENCH*?

The Clench

What's more intimidating than a blank page, a white canvas, or a spot-lit stage? It's why so few people write the books they say are inside of them. It's why so many others say their biggest fear in the world is speaking or performing in public. It's why so many canvases stay blank. The presence of fear when facing page, canvas, stage, or any other creative space yet to be filled is what I call "the clench."

What is the clench? You've probably felt it, too. For me, there is a tightening in my belly that corrupts my thinking. In the clench, I hear: "Well, you had some decent things to say yesterday, but it looks like you're all dried up today." And then, "What made you think you could write, anyway?"

The clench occurs when you are relying only on your own strength and trying too hard. It happens when you hear yourself say, "I have to make this point really well here."

Fear is always outcome focused. This fear tells me that I feel that I need to do this all by myself. It tells me that I need to control the outcome. When I am aware of the clench, it serves to remind me that if I relax my hold a little more and hold it a little lighter (not tighter), the chances of something more imaginative will come through if I let the muses speak a little.

There is a great quote from *A Course in Miracles*, a book by Helen Schucman that was published in 1976: "If you knew who walks beside you, fear would be impossible."

Who walks beside you?

The Receptive Zone

When you identify the question that you need an answer for, set it in your mind and ask for guidance from your team. Then let it go. Usually, it will come when you least expect it because you have gotten your brain out of the way. When you're in the shower, on a bike, on a train, walking in the rain, things will show up to guide you.

It can come in an 'aha!' moment, or in a trail of symbols. It can come in a whisper over your shoulder. You may stumble upon the answer when you are walking through a bookstore. "Pick me," it will say. Or, a friend may say the perfect thing that opens your mind to a fresh idea. On the internet, you will click on something that takes you to a new place. Anything can happen when you question yourself about what you want. You won't know where or how it will come from, but something will show up that will take you to an answer.

Encouragement

When you've faced your fears, discomfort, and dread enough to sit your ass down and get over them, remember to express gratefulness to yourself. Once you've felt gratitude, think about the result. Treat yourself as a child who just finished his homework. Say, "Good job—you've finished that task. How will you reward yourself?"

I'm sure that if someone could hear me talk to myself, they would think I was crazy. I talk to myself like a parent talking to a 5-year-old. "You did so good today!" Or, "It's OK, sweetie. Keep going, one step at a time."

When you get stuck as you're working, give yourself encouragement by saying, "It's OK. This is just a rough patch, so keep going. You've got this. Good job, girl. Move on to another area and come back to it. You'll figure it out."

After a session of working, whether it turned out for good or is still imperfect, be an advocate for yourself. Say, "Look at you. You had a hard day at work and you still carved out time to make some art and express yourself. You're amazing. Plan a reward for yourself when you come back here tomorrow."

There is a part of you that needs this kind of self-encouragement. Be a perfect parent to yourself. Encourage, and reward. Yes, go ahead and coddle yourself. Not everybody is being so brave in their life. You are, though.

Listen for
the *pulses...*

...not the
pings.

Healthy Deferment

It's the morning when you scheduled time to play with your *one thing* project. Let's say you have scheduled two hours. Just beyond these two hours is a list of other, practical stuff to do in this day.

You review the list and read, "The laundry." You say, "I can play in *the zone* when the laundry is all done." So, you start the laundry cycling in the machines, and then you go back to the list to see that you wrote the need to get gas…and then go to the bank. You say, "I can relax better if I've cleared up the errands."

This is normal bargaining. It makes sense. It's the certainty of doing the things you can control and you know are what take priority. For now, you can be safe and not deal with uncertainty. The uncertainty is always that creative project that lies in front of you.

So, while driving on your errands, you think about the uncertainty. "Will it go well?" "Do I know what I' m going do later today?" "Might I ruin today the good work I produced yesterday?" And, "Is there still two hours left this morning for me to go into my chamber?"

This kind of process costs you your pride and your power at the end of the day—unless you've postponed some of your tasks. When you put those tasks ahead of creativity, you only make yourself feel temporarily satisfied. Your creative life is what makes you feel fulfilled…so defer your tasks!

This is what I call a "healthy deferment." Here are four suggestions for giving yourself back to yourself:

1. **Ask yourself how you will feel at the end of those two hours when you have entered *the zone* of the playground?** Will you feel satisfied? Proud? Stimulated? Empowered? Inspired? Answering yes to all those questions is the goal. It's not the quality of creative work you've done, but the feelings you experience at the end of it.

2. **As you begin your day, imagine yourself in *the zone*.** Enrich your body with feelings of having that screenplay on the computer in your lap, breathing in the smell of fresh paint, the grace in your body when you dance. Reveling in imagining the character you're creating for the stage or the page. Engage your senses by imagining the comfort of being in that creative place.
3. **Give yourself a reward when you finish your hours of creative time.** Take a bath. Spend time with a friend. Enjoy a cup of tea or a glass of wine.
4. **Be nice to yourself.** Say, "Here you started the day unsure if you were going to write, but you did anyway. Well done, you!"

The Helpers

As in the hero's journey, all heroes have helpers show up for them. That is true of the creative's journey as well. They'll show up just when you are lost and find you don't know the next step or need to find a new class or learn a new skill. The key is to ask for help.

"I need to learn more about calligraphy."

"I want to find a studio to rent. Send help, please."

"Give me some new inspiration about how to paint the right-hand side of my canvas."

Cara was writing a book. She had never navigated writing a book before, so she was unaccustomed to the different levels of process: first draft, edit, second draft, revision, final proof, and then, querying, pitching, navigating the many worlds of publishing options. She didn't know when to stop researching, when to gather more ideas, when to start editing, or even how to know when she was done. She wrote to me about her situation:

"I was lost in a sea of good ideas in my book, but there were too many and I was confused and frustrated. I was adrift in 'idea overwhelm' and with two months to my deadline, I was feeling stressed. I asked my guidance to put the GPS on a formula or focus for getting to the next step.

"The next week I was in a coffee shop writing away and still feeling overwhelmed. A man sat next to me and asked what I was doing. He introduced himself as a ghostwriter and after listening to my struggle, offered a simple tool for focusing each chapter on my main message, which was to inspire and encourage people towards enlightened self-care. Every chapter was to be filtered through this lens. If the chapter wasn't doing its job to get people to action, it would need to be discarded or changed. It was a pivotal moment in the next step of my writing."

This man was a mystery helper for Cara and he literally showed up in the nick of time. She had asked for guidance and a helper showed up. Even though I experience this all the time in my life, I continue to still be in awe of this seemingly mystical phenomena!

Empowering Your Feelings

Every day I write my goals, appointments, and intentions. I also write what I want to get done, but in the middle of a circle, I write the intentions for how I want to feel. Some of the words that might show up in this circle are:

- Proud
- Accomplished
- Vibrant
- Whole
- Surprised
- Easy
- Delighted
- Generous
- Accepting

I write these words into the circle like I'm choosing a drop of emotional intention for the day and the energy of emotion that I want to generate.

"Feeling" types of intentions generate a higher energy field than "thought" types of intentions. At the end of the day, I go back to my journal and see if I experienced any of the feelings I'd written down in the morning. I am often amazed by how it works. For example, I love when I've written "surprised," and remember a moment in the day that caught me with delighted surprise. It reminds me that I am the architect of my day in intentional feelings, as well as tasks.

So, I care about how I feel. I tend to it like a garden. When it comes to my creative work, however, I can easily get off track when I listen to thoughts about other things I must do. My feelings about sitting down and making must be positive, free, and not tainted by logic. My commitments to my art must carry the same energy as my commitments to getting done the everyday, menial work. They must be given the same honor and respect.

People are often waylaid by the concept of art having to be led by inspiration. Yet, artists and creatives know there are days when there is no inspiration at all. The important thing is to do it anyway. Here's why. Before the scheduled creating time, it is common to hear your voice of resistance. While your resistance is a fact, and may be true, it is designed to disempower you. The correction for this is to remind yourself how you'll feel once you've spent time working on your *one thing*. Go do some art, and then say, "I didn't feel like it, and I did it anyway. I feel great. I feel confident. I didn't negotiate with myself. I keep my commitments to myself. I am worthy."

When you choose to follow the "I don't feel like it" feeling, yet you have a goal of painting for an hour each day, you will feel like you let yourself down. You let yourself become a less worthy version of yourself, and a lack of trust in yourself gets planted and starts to grow.

When you choose to follow the "I'm creating today, no matter how I feel," you grow a sense of trust in yourself; you build confidence and self-worth.

Your confidence builds exponentially when you care how you feel enough to empower yourself and just do it, without negotiation.

Interpreting Your Own Truth Signals

Bravo! Brava! You have finally given up on perfectionism. You have come to believe that doing art is not a linear process. Ideas of right and wrong in terms of creation are no longer at play with you any longer.

What do you have now?

The answer is that you are left with your own truth. You now own your truth about what is your organic, original method of making.

How did you do that? How did you connect to your own voice within? You did it through your body. You observed the sensations and feelings it so lovingly produced for you. There is great wisdom in your body. You learned to attune to its wisdom, and you've been rewarded, in both life and creativity.

Bodies are always speaking. They have two languages: "yes" and "no." You will recognize the message of your body through feelings of expansion or contraction. When a choice or action is resonating with your truth, you will experience expansive energy. You'll feel energy rising and your body getting warm. You may feel a pulling forward—a desire to move. Think of the term "warming to an idea." That is the "yesss!" of the body. You can even get "flushed with enthusiasm," or begin to "wax poetic with desire." Your body's "Hell yesss!" is a great moment. It's common for this kind of a "yes" to bring a warmth that spreads in your belly or chest. Or, it can travel upwards, causing tears of happiness.

I often get the sound of "boom" or "click" or "clunk," as if something once suspended falls into its rightful place. Something "rings true." This "yes" signals an idea that belongs with me. It just feels right. Goosebumps also send me a signal that something is true and right.

There are more subtle yesses you may experience. A slight movement of energy up the spine along the arms and shoulders. A little push forward. A nudge that feels encouraging. The quiet whispers your body gives you are always trying to get your attention.

What about the "no" signals? You know, the loud "no" as a flight-fight-freeze response when there is danger, or, when something feels inappropriate to you. You may feel repulsed and run, you may argue, or, become leaden, or turn to stone. Imagine a tight fist in your solar plexus area, or your hair rising along the upper spine and neck.

The subtle "no" signals feel like a contraction, or a drop in energy. You may feel a slight pulling away, a feeling that something is receding. You could feel a sensation of withdrawal. Your belly might tighten, or you may get a sinking feeling.

Becoming sensitive to and recognizing your unique "yes" or "no" signals—the ones that come from your own body—will help make decisions about your creativity (and decisions are constant while you're in the act of making). This sensitivity will also help you create with more authenticity and originality.

Stay In

When a weekend comes, I often experience Fear of Missing Out (FOMO). Will my friends call to invite me to meet them for a happy hour, a movie, a lunch date? What will I miss out on if I just stick to my list of errands? I feel concern about not "getting out enough," or experiencing the outside world enough. When I am burdened by FOMO, I often end the weekend by reviewing my feelings about what I did. When I feel that I allowed myself diversion and distraction, at the hands of other people's agendas, I feel that at least I didn't "miss out." FOMO hits everyone in some way, whether an obsession to keep up with social media profiles, sacrificing needed "alone time" for participation with a group, or going in for meaningless distractions. It takes work to balance your desire for the expression of self with a desire to connect with other people.

If you can balance the power of staying in (with your *one thing* project) and then rewarding yourself with genuine connection with the people you love, or, greater humanity, you tend to be happier and feel more whole. To do this balancing act takes planning and devotion to yourself, your family, your friends, and your creative work. The intention you make to serve your values of creativity and connection is what lets them feed each other in a loop of support. For instance, when I have enjoyed a quality evening out with my friends, the next day, I feel filled up with the goodness in friendship. The next day, I tend to my creative work with more presence and focus. On a night when I've chosen to stay in, I look forward to making a plan and experiencing connection with friends or family as a reward. Being present with the values of creativity or connection shapes your life—and creativity—in positive ways.

"Staying in" when you've committed to it, feels cozy and warm on a cold, rainy day. "Staying in" with your creative projects feels nourishing as well. Honor is given, time and effort is offered, inspiration is tended to.

I've noticed that when I involve my friends or family in my own goals, they are more open to being flexible with their schedules. "I'm staying in today," I tell them when they offer a plan to meet for coffee. "I'd love to meet you this evening, after I feel like I've spent a good amount of time writing." When you tell them how important something is to you, true friends and loving family members want to support you. When your friends are true, you might notice that through your commitment to your own projects, they might start new projects of their own. They may or may not say it, but you will have been an inspiration to them.

Your edge is
the place that is
just a BIT MORE
than you are
comfortable with.

Find Your Edge

Ego is uncomfortable with the flow state. Flow feels like death to the ego, which always wants you to live in the known and keep safe at all costs. But what terrible costs!

The safe place, however, is an illusion. It will keep you from reaching beyond yourself and finding your growth edge. You know the safe place's warm comfort, but you also know its limitations. You don't get to experience the rush of dopamine in your brain that squirts out when you try something new and scary. You don't get to experience that jolt of confidence and a slight expansion of your own identity. You choose the same safe experiences because you have found your groove and are comfortable. That safe place, however, is the place where dying people are pissed that they have mostly lived their lives, instead of daring to live their dreams.

I'm not advocating that you freak yourself out. I'm a proponent for a giving yourself a little stretch. The flow state is willing to take you to the edge of what you already know, and give you space to expand. It is a practice to find that sweet spot between safety and a touch beyond what you know.

Think of a time when you allowed yourself to go a little further than you had before. Remember the slight thrill in reaching just beyond your already-known state. Now ask, "Where is my next edge? Where can I stretch just a little?"

Being Willing to Not Know

To be in the flow state, you must be willing not to know. It is uncomfortable. You feel as if your ego is having a shit conniption! You must be willing to withstand the discomfort of knowing that you don't know what's going to happen next, next, or next. There are never any fixed conclusions in creativity or in life—there are only choices and possibilities.

People are multidimensional in nature. Humans only use five percent of their brain capacity because they're are not willing to explore past what they know. In order to stretch beyond the five percent and expand, you must be willing to go past what you know, to go to the edge of and beyond what feels comfortable, acceptable, and reasonable. Conventional (non-creative) reasoning prefers that everyone must do things in an agreed upon manner at an agreed upon time. That's what civilized society is built on.

Compare having a creative mindset to going on a self-planned vacation. In a new country, you can allow yourself to have random conversations, be curious about the culture, and explore venues that you normally avoid when you are home. You can dance to different rhythms than to the music you are used to, and you feel more alive than when you're in familiar territory. You must use your wits to navigate the logistics, sometimes by the seat of your pants, or with a wing and a prayer! In the end, you'll be grateful for the flexibility you've built in for the surprises that will become extraordinary memories.

Now, take another kind of trip—the kind that is pre-planned by an agency. Say it's a trip to Europe on a package deal where everything has been planned out to the minute. You know where you're going to sleep, what you will see, what you will eat. You'll stick with your known traveling companions and never have to get mixed up with the foreigners. You'll never have to use your wits, intuition, and ingenuity to find your way or open your mind. The photos you take on this trip will look very similar to the ones taken by everyone else who's with you. If you want your creative journey to be like this, just stay home! Pretend you never heard the call for adventure in the first place.

Making art is akin to the experiences you have on any self-planned adventure. Anything can happen, and everyone and everything you encounter seems put here just to inspire, delight, or educate you. Sometimes, angels show up just when you need them.

The life of your project
will be revealed to be more
interesting than you.

*Yes, your creativity is more
interesting than you are.*

It takes on a life of its own
when you get out of the way.

A Life of its Own

Here's an unexpected payoff of creativity: The life of your project will be more interesting than you are.

Yes, your creativity is more interesting than you. It takes on a life of its own when you get out of the way. In the process, it will grow you in ways you had no idea you could grow. It will teach you who you are in ways that will be unexpected. It will expand your sense of self and add layers to your identity. Your *one thing* has a life of its own when you get out of its way.

How it all starts is never how it turns out.

Enter as an innocent, armed with a little curiosity, and see what can happen. Have a beginner's mind filled with nothing but questions. Better questions bring richer results.

The Better Question Game: Use your journal to ask a simple question about something you're curious about. Write what comes up as an answer.

After a few days, write that 'ask' again, but better. And by better, I mean in an expanded, more creative way. Compare the answers to both questions. Any surprises? Examples:

1st Question: "What do I love about clay?"

2nd Question: "What do I love more: working with clay on a potter's wheel or sculpting it by hand?"

1st Question: "What is being revealed to me about the female protagonist in my play?"

2nd Question: "How can I know the character I'm creating in a deeper way?"

1st Question: "What is emerging on this new canvas I've just begun to paint?"

2nd Question: "If I use more cerulean and a palette knife, what will emerge in this corner of the canvas?"

This exercise can help reveal how you are evolving through this project
as well as what the project is evolving into—through you.

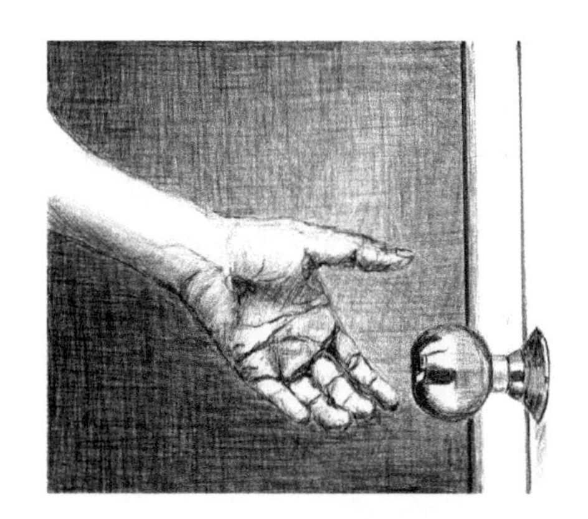

EROS is whatever
makes you come alive.
Bring that aliveness
into your lovemaking,
the making of your art,
and the making of your life.

The Mad, Wild Thing

Just like heroes in some fantastical journey, as artists we come upon forces within ourselves daily that require a decisive victory of courage. And, we do this just to counter the voices of the Impeccable Artist or the ego's fear. We know it requires heroic efforts.

There were days when you felt the power within you because you were terrified…then you became courageous. You sent in your work and then were terrified of rejection. You dared to speak the truth, and then worried about the cost. Perhaps you were terrified but then found a brave new way into uncharted territory. There were days when the best thing you did was sit down to write for an hour despite being terrified. The reason you feel terrified is because it matters. Really matters.

Courageous moments change your life. Such change can feel like you've been trapped, like a single bird in a cage, but on release you become a thousand white birds flying free, out in the air. The aftermath of a moment of great courage is awe inspiring. That's why happy, mad, wild dances were invented—they let the body express feelings of freedom!

The more you have these moments, the more you want more of them. The more you have them, the more you will snicker at those moments of terror you have, because the mad, wild thing of bravery is too sweet. Those moments of terror are the way into the mad, wild thing.

Your challenges are
the very things that
force you to dig deeper.
Courage exists
because of fear.

PART FOUR: THE OBSTRUCTION ARMY

The Obstruction Army does not want you to shine. The soldiers in this army (under the guise of keeping you safe) will appear in a variety of forms. Learning to identify, disable, and develop strategies for conquering them is a prerequisite for any creative.

The Arms Strategy

Just as the Impeccable Artist tries to derail your making and acts of creativity, when it comes to "shining" (sharing or delivering your work out in the world) there is a whole new battle to contend with. You must confront the Obstruction Army.

Like Ivan the Terrible, with his droopy eye and suspicious glare, the commander of this army, leads a team of soldiers, armed and ready to obstruct your efforts just as you are ready to reveal your work to others. His goal is to make sure no good works of beauty, innovation, or inspiration are to be put into the world. He knows that the makers, the creators, and the joy bringers are threatening to the status-quo. This army he leads knows that the collective history and culture of the world's peoples are contained in art.

Art shapes ideas, provides humanity with a deeper understanding of the emotions, and enables self-awareness. Through art, people are unified across the globe.

This is completely unacceptable to the Obstruction Army.

They view art as subversive and possibly disruptive to the status quo. Hey, who do you think burnt the books? After all, the symbols and ideas in art can engage with the world to change the world, one person at a time. The act of making lets you learn to cherish your intuition and search for new ideas. The mere process of art aims to break the rules and find new ways to approach the new possible in society.

The Obstruction Army wants to keep the collective heart quiet.

They have developed a strategy for doing so. Have you experienced the underhanded effects of this strategy yourself?

Their strategy: To convince you that they are keeping you safe from the ridicule of others.

How? By capitalizing on your primal evolutionary herd behavior, which tells you to make decisions based on the beliefs, behaviors, and choices of others.

You can take the human out of Stone Age, but you can't take the Stone Age out of the human. Unfortunately, what worked as cave people doesn't necessarily work in the 21st century, unless of course, you are running from a tiger.

The fears the Obstruction Army capitalizes on will have you concerned with possible abandonment from your tribe, exploiting your deepest need for safety and approval—all so that you will stay silent and keep your creations safely in the closet or under the bed.

Genius strategy. Right?

The Soldiers of Fear

If you are aware of the voices that are trying to put you or your work down (and not internalizing or identifying with them), hats off to you! You probably don't need this book.

For the rest of us, we listen to and evaluate these voices. Maybe we have 50 percent knowledge that they are speaking bullshit, but the other 50 percent of our knowledge identifies with them.

By what measure do you believe those voices are wrong, and how much do you let them disempower you and ruin the momentum of your creative process?

These soldiers are sneaky and devilish but are disguised as helpful. They want you to think it's for your own good. They are covert yet relentless. They want you to know that you will not be safe or accepted if you express yourself and share it boldly with others. Or, they want to give you other messages of 'not enough-ness.' They will take it up a notch and shake your confidence when you think about sending your work out into the world.

There are some common fears that show up when you think about putting your work out there. In order to face your fears, identify them and call them out. You will notice they can easily blend into each other. Here are the main soldiers of fear that most artists face, as well as the thoughts that tend to drive them:

Soldier # 1: Fear of Being Revealed as a Fraud (Impostor Syndrome)

You doubt your accomplishments and have a fear of being exposed as a fraud. You'll think:

"If I show my work to others, it will be revealed that I am not really worthy."

"Who am I to do this?"

"People are going to find out eventually that I don't know what I'm doing."

"I may not know what I'm really doing."

"People will know that I'm not really______."

"What if I'm not really creative?"

"I'm afraid I don't have anything worthwhile to say."

"Who am I to publish a book?"

"Other people have researched and done or said this better than me."

Soldier # 2: Fear of Persecution

You believe you'll be ill-treated; that you'll experience hostility and take abuse from others. Some form of harm will eventually occur:

"If I show my work to others, they will hurt me."

"My work will cause others pain and they will retaliate."

"I'm afraid I could get crucified in public."

"If I show this side of me, my career could be ruined."

"If my sister reads this, she would be so hurt."

"My whole family will resent me forever."

Soldier # 3: Fear of Exposure

You believe if your mask of invulnerability slips (like when you become vulnerable and tell the truth) there may be rejection, shame, or abandonment. You'll hear your inner voice say:

"If I show my work to others, they will know my unworthiness and see that I am imperfect."

"If I tell the truth about myself and reveal my soft underbelly, people will shame me."

"I will look too ___foolish/weak/amateur/____."

"If I tell what I really think or show this side of me, people will see the real me and abandon me."

"If people judge me for what comes out, I will have to face that I am really not worthy, not good, not loveable."

Soldier # 4: Fear of Lack of Originality

You believe your work lacks value in the eyes of others. It may be judged for a lack of inventiveness or distinctiveness. Do any of the following statements sound familiar?

"If I show my work to others, it may be perceived as having been copied or imitated in some way."

"This has already been done. I'm not offering anything new here."

"I don't think I have anything new to say."

"Everything I have to say is stuff everyone already knows."

"Everything I'm doing is just a rehash of old ideas."

"I'm afraid I'm not expressing anything exceptional."

"I don't really have a fresh voice; I was influenced by ____."

"Why would anyone want to read this when they have heard this before?"

Soldier # 5: Fear of Judgment

You fear "not being enough;" either not 'good enough,' or being 'too much.' This fear of judgment is always linked to the desire to be liked and approved of. Fear of judgment sounds like:

"If I show my work, I will not be liked or approved of by my friends, family and others I respect."

"I'm afraid that everyone will hate it."

"I'm afraid it is going to make someone mad."

"What if it's laughed at?"

"What if they think I'm stupid?"

"What if my friends see it and hate it and then snicker behind my back?"

Soldier # 6: Fear of Imperfection

You fear showing flaws or defects to others. You need to be certain to make your work faultless in order to be irreproachable. You say:

"If I show my work before it is impeccable, I will be seen as unworthy and not a consummate artist."

"I'm afraid people will think my writing is bad."

"I'm afraid it won't be perfect."

"What if my standards are too low for the marketplace?"

"What if it's too complicated for others to understand?"

"I'm afraid I didn't work hard enough."

"I'm afraid I'm going to forget everything I should say."

"I'm afraid I might quit before it's fully complete, then I'll feel like a loser."

"I'm afraid I put too much in."

"People could think I'm a terrible painter."

"My sloppy style is not marketable."

When you take a steady and mature look at these common fears, each soldier shares a common theme. They share the piercingly vulnerable current of:

FEAR ABOUT WHAT OTHERS THINK ABOUT YOU.

Boil all the fears down to the one element that keeps you from shining to let it reveal these cardboard cut-out soldiers! Break it down like this to feel relief that you can do something simple to neutralize the soldiers' control over you. You'll not need to see your fear as a complex psychological condition to solve with therapy.

All these fears are projected judgments of what you think someone else might believe—a belief you don't like! So, in effect, your worries, like the cardboard cut-out soldiers, are imaginary.

If your fears about what others might think about you are imaginary, then why should you allow them to keep you small, sheltered, hidden? Imaginary fears will keep you on the couch and stop you from doing *the one thing* that will change your life for the better. Is the shame spiral of you never doing the *one thing* that is calling you worth it? Is missing out of feeling happy and proud that you were in the minute percentage of people who wrote a book and published it worth shying away from judgements made by others?

When you put your attention on what others think of you, it puts you into a state of self-consciousness. There is nothing less creative than being self-conscious and judgmentally self-aware. If you find yourself watching through the eyes of someone else, which is common when you are forming a new and healthy identity as an artist, you know you are in the grip of fear of some type of judgement. It is impossible to shine when you are waiting for judgement to fall on your head.

Creativity is very sensitive to possible censorship. The irony is that in order to express your creativity in *the zone*, you must bypass your critical mind and get vulnerable. The minute you think about pressing "publish," organizing an art gallery opening, or performing your poems in public, you freak out. You get paralyzed. You can't bear the thought of being" too open" or "too vulnerable." You might even try to make yourself invisible. You fear disapproval because you think it will threaten your security or self-worth. You avoid taking any risks because the thoughts of judgment, failure, or disapproval terrifies you. You hand your power over to some imaginary projection of a worst-case scenario involving an imaginary outcome.

These soldiers of fear are every artist's cross to bear, and common to the point of cliché. Every artist needs to navigate their way through them their own way by developing new perspectives, values, and skills for coping with them if they want to shine.

Forget searching
for “originality”
in your art. True
originality is in the
tension between your
curiosity and convention.

Catch Them Red-Handed

When you can catch the obstruction army in the act: "Why on earth would you think you can paint?" "Who made you the king of rock and roll?" you can employ techniques of cognitive behavior therapy by imagining a huge red STOP sign that says, "NO! You may not pass here," like you are Gandalf at the gates. Besides creating a symbol of the image of the stop sign that the brain interprets as NO, it begins to know you mean business and can redirect itself. The mere fact that you are noticing these destructive thoughts means you are no longer operating in auto-monkey-mind. It is a reason to celebrate.

Rejoice, fellow human, you have just added years to your happiness quotient, so celebrate and reward your brain. Say, "I'm noticing! Hurrah!"

If you are sensitive enough to notice your voices of obstruction yammering at you, you know your sensitivity for your voices of inspiration to be increasing as well! This is major creative progress. You are expanding. You are developing a higher-tuned frequency and are no longer the victim of repetitive thought patterns. This is huge good news.

By doing the happy dance, you are also signaling to your brain that this is important to the system. You just set the GPS of your brain to a higher frequency and this means you no longer are a victim of your thoughts.

CELEBRATE! Say, "YESSS! I AM NOTICING!" Know that your energy flows where your attention goes. The hardest part of any art is learning to defeat the Army of Obstruction. You can learn painting or dance or acting until the cows come home, but you won't create any sustainability in your work until you learn to defeat the destructiveness that tears you and your work apart.

Tender Hearts Exposed

It's all fine and good to get into *the zone* and make your *one thing*. After all, this is your baby. But it's a whole other ball of buggers when thinking about putting your baby out into the world, knowing that you or it may be judged.

The more heart you've put into your making, the further you've reached out of your comfort zone. The more it matters to you, the riskier it can feel to open it up to external critics. Creativity can feel very personal and can leave you feeling vulnerable when you show it to others.

Here are some common fears my clients have expressed when preparing to expose themselves publicly:

"People could know things about me that I am too embarrassed to reveal."

"I would be seen for the insecure, flawed person I really am."

"I would no longer be allowed to hide behind my mask of perfection."

What if you view fear as a healthy body signal for you to stop and re-group? Give yourself a little snap on the wrist with a rubber band to pay attention and process for a minute. How do you do this? First, feel the paralysis fear brings as it stops your ride. Ask it questions. Show it gratitude. Feel it relaxing. Release it with love. Begin to move again as you leave The State Of Your Fears behind.

Rather than getting stuck in the fear, reconnect to why it matters, and what it makes possible. Use that as fuel to push through the fear. The fear that being truthful about your life frailties and vulnerabilities will have others recoil in horror and shock or piss off your family members is like a creative muzzle.

The cost is profound. You are telling yourself on some level that your story, your experience is shameful and should be silenced. You deny yourself the right to speak your truth. You deny others the right to connect to your story which may be healing and empowering to them.

Art is a unifier. A connector. An avenue to have us all feel less alone in an isolating world.

My client, Carrie, is an example of someone terrified to share her heart (and art) due to those soldiers of fear. Her experience, when she finally did share it, was inspiring.

Carrie had a son who was an addict. She helped herself process her emotions through writing in her journal. Her words were powerful and deeply felt and her writing was forceful. When I encouraged her to start publishing her work, she recoiled in horror. She feared others would judge her parenting style and she felt shame for her possible perceived role in her son's addiction. When she released the shame of other people's reactions to her experience and used the mantra, 'What other people believe about me is not my business,' something in her shifted. She began to think of her words as a possible way to reach out to other parents of kids with addictions. She finally published her writings and to her surprise, began to develop a following. A community of support came together. This is so often how it starts once someone gives up the shame of exposure.

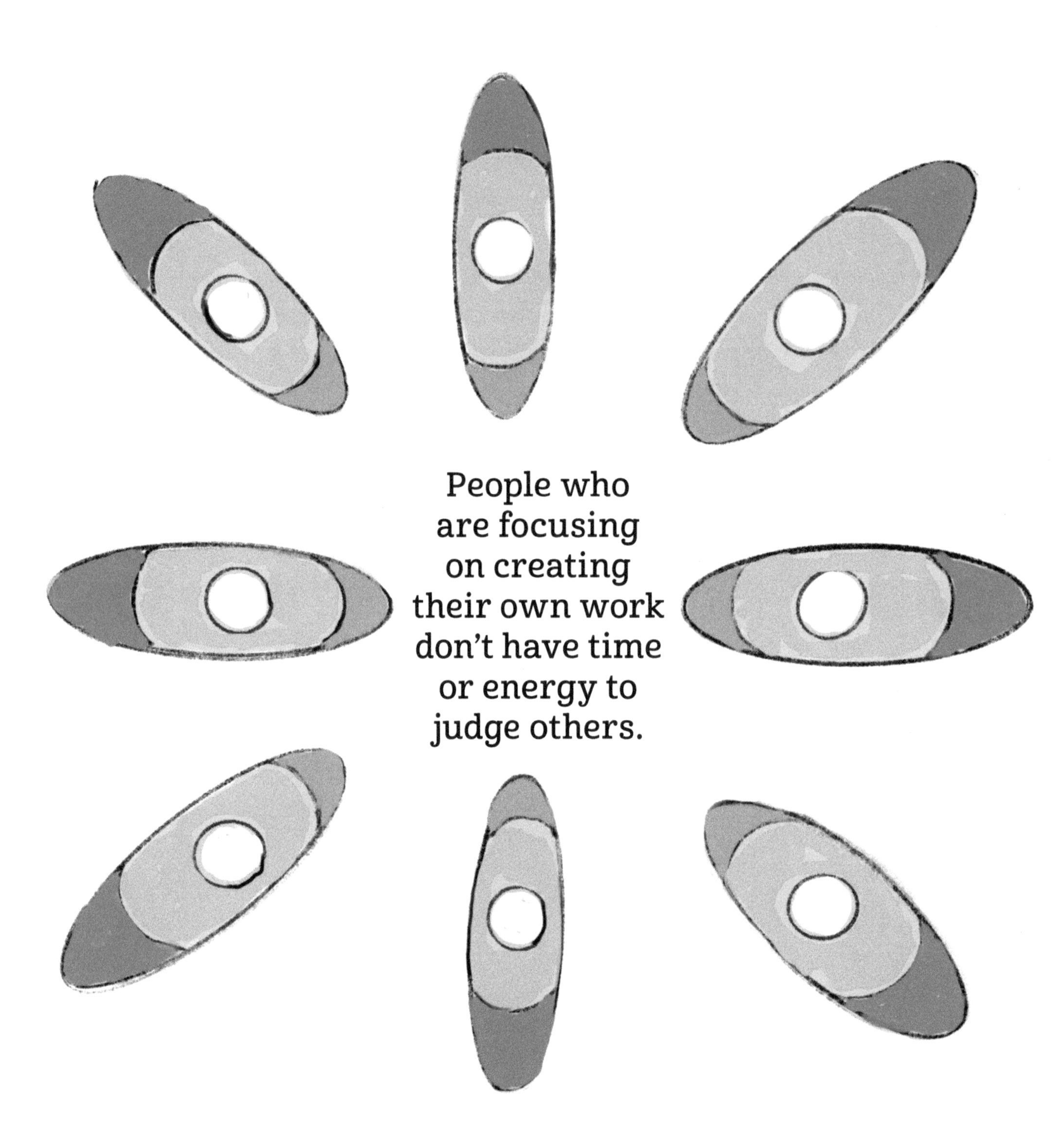
People who
are focusing
on creating
their own work
don't have time
or energy to
judge others.

People Will Talk

No single piece or type of art will please everybody. Art, beauty, love, and creativity are all subjective!

When it comes to the fear of your work being rejected or criticized, conventional wisdom tells you, "Don't take it personally." How can you not, though? When you have opened your heart and soul, had the courage to make something, put it out in the world, and have it criticized—it's painful. That work felt like your baby—and now you feel as if you've sent it off to the slaughterhouse.

The truth is, the fact is, you will be rejected and criticized by some people. You just will. Yet there is something freeing about knowing that. You don't have to waste energy and brain cells trying to figure out how to please everybody.

Your job as a creative person isn't to be accepted by everybody. Your job is to make art. Your job is to keep making better art. And, your job is to speak your truth and share it. Not everyone is going to love or even like it. If you mold your message or artistic expression in the direction where you think you will be accepted, you will still be rejected by some. So then, you've sold your soul to the devil and watered down your uniqueness. Those who do not resonate with your work have nothing to do with you.

Tell yourself, "That comment had nothing to do with me." By saying this, you create a power stance which helps you stay in your own lane and curate the general estimate of between 60,000 to 80,000 thoughts that swirl around your brain in a single day.

People will talk, and the more you shine your work out there and make from your soul, the more people will talk about you. Some of them will want to tear you down. Some of them will be threatened by you and will do things to demean you.

Be very glad. It means you are making an impact.

As Oscar Wilde said, "There is only one thing worse than being talked about, and that is not being talked about."

Negative publicity is still publicity…attention! The sting you feel will be over in a minute, but the fact that you are causing waves means you have influenced someone. You can never control how someone reacts to your work; their perception is on them. What you can do is manage your own reaction with neutrality. Navigate the transition by turning the "negative" (i.e. "They don't like my work") into productive and optimistic attitudes such as:

"I'm speaking through my art."

"I'm making an impact."

"I've given them something uncomfortable to feel or think about."

"Well, my art is certainly getting some attention."

You have no control over others; not in what they think, how they feel, or what they say. When you get caught up in doing what others think you should do, you allow yourself to get attached to their outcome. You end up giving them control.

Eleanor Roosevelt said, "What other people think of me is none of my business," and that attitude is a powerful tool for creatives. She knew that when you are obsessed with what other people think, you prevent yourself from reaching your true potential and realizing your dreams.

So, put your attention where it belongs. Put it on those who resonate with your work. They are the ones who really have something to do with you.

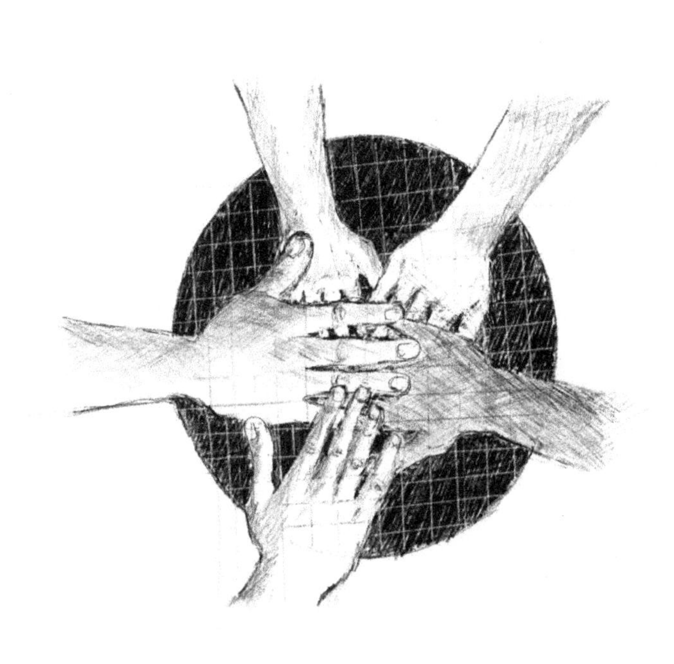

Don’t let the
perfect be the
enemy of the
POSSIBLE.

Where Perfection Hides Out

The single biggest block or obstruction to creativity is perfectionism. It is the Impeccable Artist's favorite tool to defeat your creativity. Perfection is tricky, like a complicated psychological diagnosis. It is disguised as many things. It presents as many things and it is present in every person's body. The cost of perfectionism is profound. It robs you of being present. Perfectionism pushes you into the future, where you know you'll be judged. Under perfectionism's guise of discernment and high standards is a pervasive search for lack and insufficiency.

Perfectionism also robs you of your playful enthusiasm and enjoyment, which is central to all creativity. It supposes you need to be serious in order to affect any greatness, which is false. There is a difference between the delicious single focus that comes when you are emerged in a project and the attitude of seriousness.

Your Impeccable Artist wants things already done, and to be "great." Therefore, perfectionism keeps you from starting anything. It takes away your freedom to make mistakes. It prevents you from making discoveries and finding your unique style or voice. It robs you of beginning. It will tell you that you can make a move to begin only when you are ready; it robs you of your time—time when you could be using your own life force for good. Perfectionism whisks away your innocence. Because perfectionism searches through the lens of criticism (what's wrong, what won't work, what is flawed), it tends to make you cynical. Most critics are cynical. But then, they aren't doing anything. They are only pointing their fingers.

Perfectionism denies you the pleasure of the process of doing, and all the learning that's inherent in creating. Perfectionism insists that you "should" do it "right," or not do it at all.

Nobody has ever thrived in perfectionism's model.

Perfectionism may be what is stalling you from beginning your *one thing*.

You may want to discover where your perfectionism tends to hide. Everyone has their own brand of perfectionism. Be a sleuth and find your perfectionism by answering the following questions:

"Do I feel a need to prove myself?"

"Do I like to know more than others?"

"Do I have a desire to control others?"

"Do I like to explain the most efficient way or the best way to do things?"

"Do I feel the need to be in control of my time?"

"Do I have a low tolerance for failure—in myself or in others?"

"Am I afraid to make a mistake?"

"Am I more worried about doing things right, or doing the right things?"

"Do I prefer things to be neat and tidy?"

"Do I believe people learn from mistakes?"

"Would I rather be right or happy?"

Shine Anyway

In the face of judgement from yourself or others, just know you will live. It hurts, it's annoying, it's terrible, yet you can still use it. You can make a choice to not collapse your space in the face of criticism. Make a choice to not make the criticism bigger than you. It can crush you or make you stronger. It can provide a source of amusement or be a resource for leaning even further into your truths. You can learn from it or reject it summarily. You have a choice.

You may use judgement to expand and keep creating, knowing your work is only a microcosm of what will keep coming through you. Because you, unlike the haters, are at least doing your *one thing*.

I admire the stance that Brené Brown finally adopted in her own life after much public criticism. She figures if the "judgers" aren't doing the hard, vulnerable work of risking putting themselves out there like she is, she simply will not give them the power to judge her. This is a very empowering stance; to summarily dismiss the judgers if they aren't playing on the ball field too. After all, it's so much easier to be sitting on the sidelines.

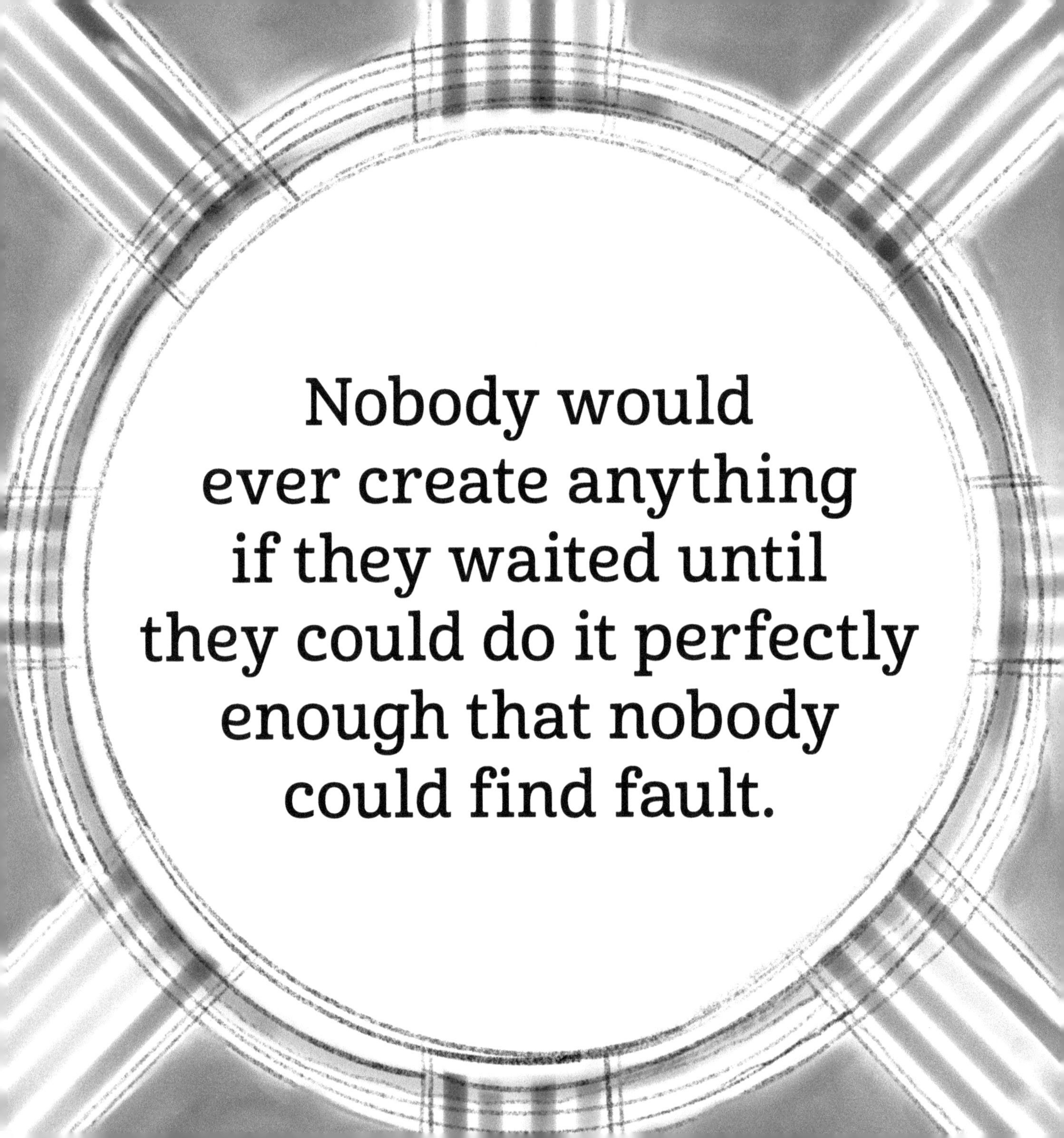
Nobody would
ever create anything
if they waited until
they could do it perfectly
enough that nobody
could find fault.

But It's Supposed to be Easy

Wait. Who says it's supposed to be easy? Of course, you know that doing anything of value isn't necessarily going to be easy, but "knowing" that, and fighting against your need for pleasure and safety is—well—it's damn hard.

People say relationships are "hard." Substitute "effort" for the idea behind the word "hard." Or, think about the active use of energy (which may be "easy" but it still requires effort) in producing any result. That's because relationships, like art, take effort to keep them vital and sustainable. I like to compare having a good relationship with another person to the relationship you want to have with your creativity. Both types of relationships take effort, but they are both so worth the energy.

Nobody likes thinking about effort. Effort can mean discomfort. Effort means breaking patterns, looking inward, taking ownership, doing things you're not used to. Effort means you could be wrong, get lost, must solve problems. But effort is where substance and depth live—not in ease.

Easy has its own purpose! Easy always feels good—but you need to understand it. It can be like the effects of sugar—temporary and addictive, a quick fix to get you over an obstacle. Or, ease can provide a bit of rest in your process—like a drink of cold water to quench the thirst you built from expending energy. But most important, ease and effort create ceilings and floors in your room without walls—necessary boundaries—that enhance your understanding of your art and its reasons, joys, and process.

If you want something easy that feels good all the time, it's as useless as the idea that art is only accomplished by exerting tremendous effort. Without ease and effort, there is no great journey. Without a journey, there is no growth.

Being with Fear

Fear is one thing that all artists who are preparing to shine will experience. Fear can show many faces

These fears are to be expected at this level of your artistic game. You can deny, hide, pretend, resist, push down, and suppress them, but they will always find a way to get your attention until you stop and feel them, hear what they have to say. To be felt is fear's primary mission. Fear wants and needs to be seen. I often wonder if people are more afraid of how they will be while feeling fear, than when they are actually experiencing it.

Here is the way you define yourself in fear: "I am afraid." And, here is the way to avoid defining yourself as fearful: "I am being in fear." Do you see the difference? By identifying as afraid—you are. By saying what you're "being," it gives you a nanosecond of choice to jump out and "be" something else.

When you face "being" in fear, it gives your sense of self a disconnect from the identity of being a fearful person. It brings acceptance to the condition without becoming it. There is nothing wrong with you—you are being. You are not broken—you are being. You are not separate—you are being.

Every artist who is preparing to shine is going through some version of fear. You are not alone. It takes courage to be in "being" with your fear, rather than identifying with it as a part of yourself.

Being present with fear instead of full of fear is a creative way to deal with the experience of fear.

Shine It Out and They Will Come

It's perfectly wondrous to use your making to please yourself—to heal, to give to family and friends, to use creative expression to settle your nervous system and de-stress, to find communities of other people with which to bond. Art has so many possibilities and offers so many gifts.

When you want to put your art out in the world, it's like moving up to the next level of a video game. To have it be seen, to gain a following, or sell it, to publish it, have it performed or displayed is to shine it out and risk criticism, rejection, and ridicule. You and your art must expect to go on a hero's journey.

Everyone has an opinion about art. Everyone has their own unique preferences. If you want to please everybody, you defeat the purpose of creative expression. You lose the game.

A client of mine had recently written a piece about her mother's death and read it to her memoir writers' group. She had thrown her heart and soul into it. The response of the group was underwhelming to say the least. When we spoke, she repeatedly expressed her disappointment.

"I don't know why they didn't like it. I worked so on this so hard and I did not get one positive response."

I replied, "I'm noticing the energy you are putting into other people's responses to your work."

"Well, I think everybody cares a little," she said.

"What was it like for you to write this piece about your mother's death?"

"Oh, it was really cathartic. I felt like I had healed something in me by writing it." she said, her voice lifting in energy.

"Would you take that experience away from yourself by filtering your work through the lens of other people's possible reactions?"

After our conversation she decided to pursue publishing her piece despite the lukewarm attention her group gave her. She sent the piece off to her editor. Days later she received an email from the editor expressing wholeheartedly how much reading the piece meant to her, having just lost her own mother. She gave recommendations for my client about possible publishing avenues for people experiencing grief and loss.

You and your art are like a lighthouse. When you make and express from your heart, then put it out into the world, you will naturally find a group of people who find your light and resonate with what you put out there. All of us are living in a unique time where we can reach a large swath of people more easily through the internet: social media venues, blogs, and websites. Technology has made the world smaller. The internet is where it is possible for you to find a group of like-minded people to share your passions with. It is an exciting time to be alive in terms of your output being received. Your tribe will be found. You can use art's subjectivity to your advantage.

In this smaller world, the possibilities are broader. The original intent and vibration of your artistic efforts will find its equivalent reception.

The Show-Up, Not the Show-Off

There are those people (and we all know them) who find an identity they like to project about themselves onto others, such as a romantic version of "artist." They like the way it sounds when they say things like, "I'm working on writing a musical," or "I'm getting ready for an art show," "Oh yeah, my band and I are recording an album." They hang their hats on how it sounds to others and build an identity around that. Others are impressed; then they feel good about their projected identities, but no work actually gets done. Meanwhile, the energy they could invest into actually doing the work is put into what I see as showing off. It's a terrible waste of energy. (It's like complaining about your problems and blowing off just enough steam to keep yourself from solving them.) The talkers are more interested in being seen as interesting, rather than cultivating a curious interest that guides their life. They are more interested in their identity (ego's satisfaction) rather than getting fulfillment from the interests they cultivate. These are the "show-offs."

In contrast, people who are "show-ups" let their work speak for itself. They don't brag or have to prove anything to others. In fact, there is a natural humility in those who show up to something bigger than themselves—their *one thing*. There is something about the way they devote themselves to an art form or project that is infinitely more interesting than their egos.

You are a "show-up" because you have a dream to explore something. Use the dream/intention as an excuse to go on the journey. Enjoy what you are doing, by doing what you're doing. While you know you will be changed by the process, it is not about your identity. This is not about showing off your result. It's about using the creative process as a rock tumbler for your evolution. The irony is that you will become more interesting as a result.

The daily consistency you create and intentions you make are the things that allow your dream to come to fruition. Be in involvement. Be amazed. Have confidence in yourself to evolve.

Like a video game, at every different level of creativity the rules and/or needed skills change. The constant is you. Keep adapting to the different levels and keep your heart engaged. And play! Play this game!

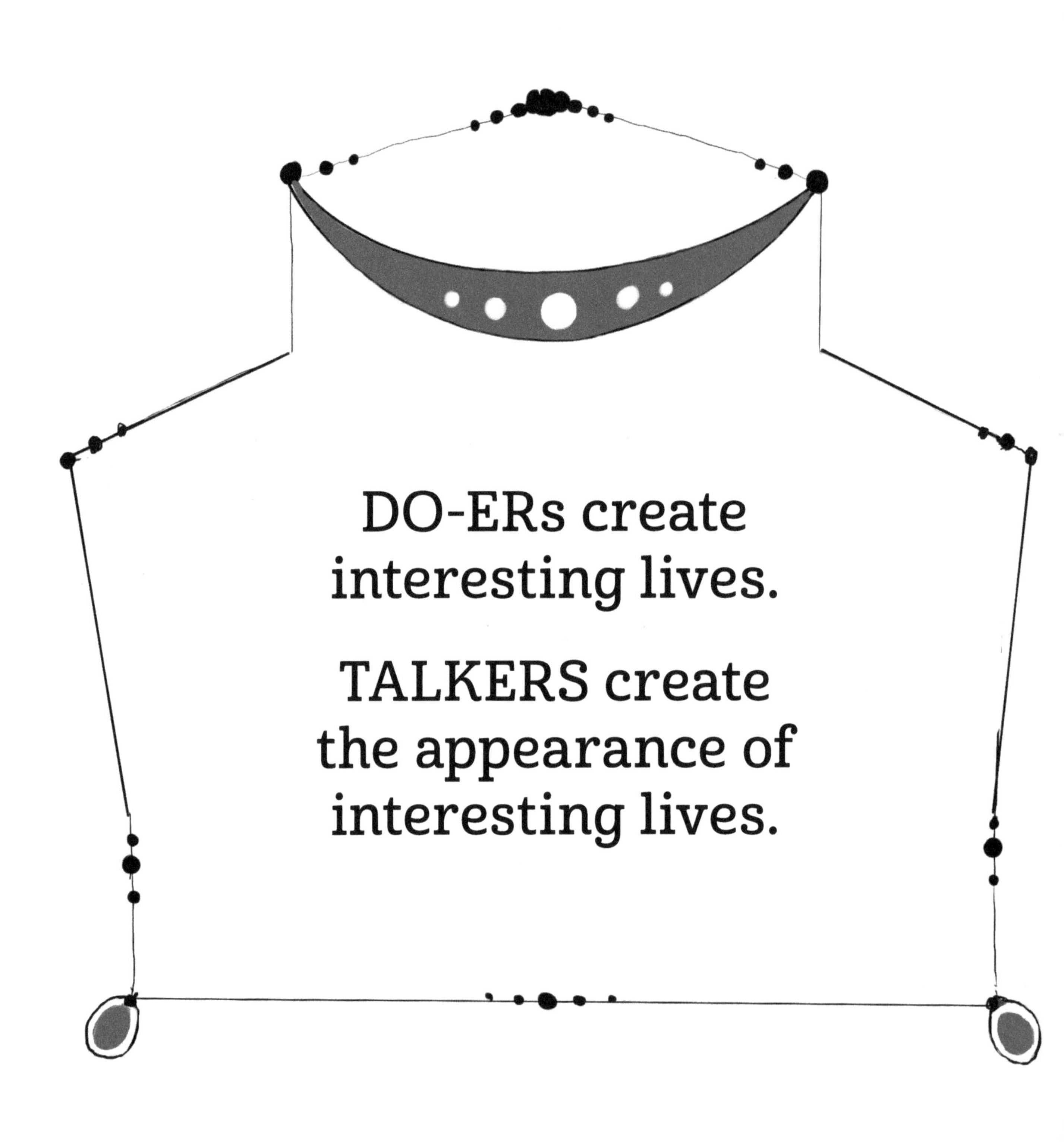
DO-ERs create
interesting lives.
TALKERS create
the appearance of
interesting lives.

But Am I Any Good?

Everyone worries about whether they are "any good" at their chosen art form.

Did you have a traumatic experience with a teacher who shamed or discouraged you during class? You might have heard, "A sky is not purple. You should make it blue." Did you hear someone laugh at or judge your finished product? "That's a cat? She told me it was a cat! Come on…it looks like a donkey!"

Still, everyone has a desire for expression, and to be understood. You may attempt to suppress your desires and longings in order to avoid the discomfort of judgement. Therefore, you must be willing to make some bad art in order to let your body learn how to both handle criticism and use it to make better art. If you dare to put your head on the chopping block and risk being seen at the early stages of entering your creative fire, prepare to be seen as sloppy, unsure, tentative, and inept. This is the way you take the first wobbly steps of your hero's journey.

When you allow your curiosities to take the lead and continue showing up, you must follow the curves and turns and accept the challenges. That is how you uncover something unique and original.

The question, "Am I any good?" is really a lousy question.

The better questions are:

"Who will I be after I go through this fire?"

"What is trying to emerge here?"

"What's the next level of my game?"

"What am I learning here?"

The Soul Loves
a Noble and
Worthy Struggle.

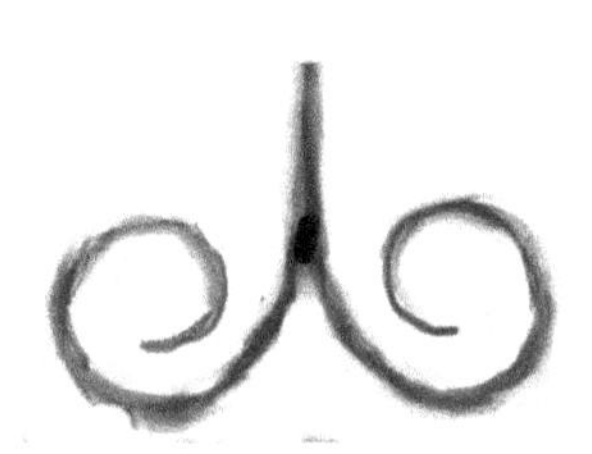

Trouble in the Tunnel

There is a stage in the middle of the creative process that is lonely, painful, and hard. This stage resembles being stuck inside a dark tunnel where ahead you can't see any light at the end, and behind you, there is no light of remembrance for what made you even start in the first place. There might be the sound of something scurrying around you, it's muddy, you can't see a thing, and it's cold and dank as hell in there. You've lost the joy and the spark of the adventure of this journey. You have lost heart.

I believe the tunnel stage is why about 80 percent of books started, eventually get slid into a drawer, unfinished.

Creatively, it could look like overwhelm in the possible passageways in the tunnel; too many challenging options, ideas, more and more decisions to make, not enough time or information available. Trouble could show up as too many papers, too much research, blocking the light at the end. You could have skill set or technology blockages of rubble that need to be cleared away before any more progress through can be made. You could feel frustration with the pace of your progress and want to sit on your haunches leaning against the dank walls. Or, your negative thoughts have taken up residence and are chewing on the creation like rats.

The middle stage may make you feel paralyzed. You see a mess and you don't know how to get out of it. You look at the work and decide it's shite. You want to quit. This is a normal event in the life of a project and can be debilitating for an artist.

Women creatives, mothers who've experienced giving birth, will likely relate to this idea. For others, you should know that during childbirth, there is a phase where the mother wants to shout, "Forget it! I'm not doing this anymore. This is more than I can bear. This is stupid!" In the throes of what her body is doing (and what must be done), she blames all her discomfort on the father, the professional birthing staff, and anyone else who is present. She is in a transition between holding onto her creation and letting it go, and it comes with pain, doubt, frustration, and utter misery.

Here are six suggestions for the "trouble in the tunnel" phase:

1. **Evaluate the costs of quitting.** When I was in the tunnel, frustrated and lacking in confidence, I confessed to a wise and trusted friend, "Look, maybe I don't actually want to write a book after all." She looked at me levelly and said, "Well, what would happen if you just quit?" I returned her steady gaze. First there was a feeling of a relief (because I wouldn't have to experience all this anxiety anymore). Then, I was alarmed (because "How dare she act so nonchalant? This was my *one thing*!") In that one moment of having it taken away, I was able to gain clarity in order to decide. "If I quit, I will lose complete respect for myself. I will regret it. No, I'm going to finish," I said. After that day, my energy was restored. I was able to charge on through, finishing the first draft in three weeks' time. I'm not saying that there are not times when projects need to be set aside for a while, or abandoned completely to start another, more vital one. What I'm suggesting is to maneuver through the middle of the tunnel, it is helpful to ask yourself what the ultimate costs would be if you quit?
2. **Reflect on the beginning.** Look behind you at how far you've come. Remember the beginning? That enthusiasm or curiosity that you experienced when you first started your project? See the qualities and skills that you already possess, or you have acquired, that have gotten you here so far. Offer some acceptance to yourself. Have gratitude for your qualities of showing up and having the courage to create.
3. **Notice who you have become now.** Were you the same person when you started as you are now? See how this has grown you so far. Who will you be when you come to the end of this road with this project? Enjoy the wonder of it. Notice and appreciate your growth.

Re-commit to taking things chunk by chunk, step by step, decision by decision. Remind yourself that perfection is not interesting or unique.

4. **Notice how the field is changing.** You can't see the end yet, but you are still on the road. Remember that YOU are the constant here. The project will keep evolving and all you need to do is keep adapting. Have confidence to let the process keep unfolding and know that you will have the confidence to let it evolve.
5. **Send encouragement to other tunnel travelers.** Know that you are not alone. There are many who have been on this journey and are going through it now. The tunnel is a required passage check- point for all creative travelers. Send them some encouragement as you offer yourself the same.
6. **Know that this too will pass.** After you get through this period, it's going to get smoother. Have faith. It's going to get easier as soon as you travel through a little further. Soon you can proudly report that you've been there, done that, and bought the t-shirt.

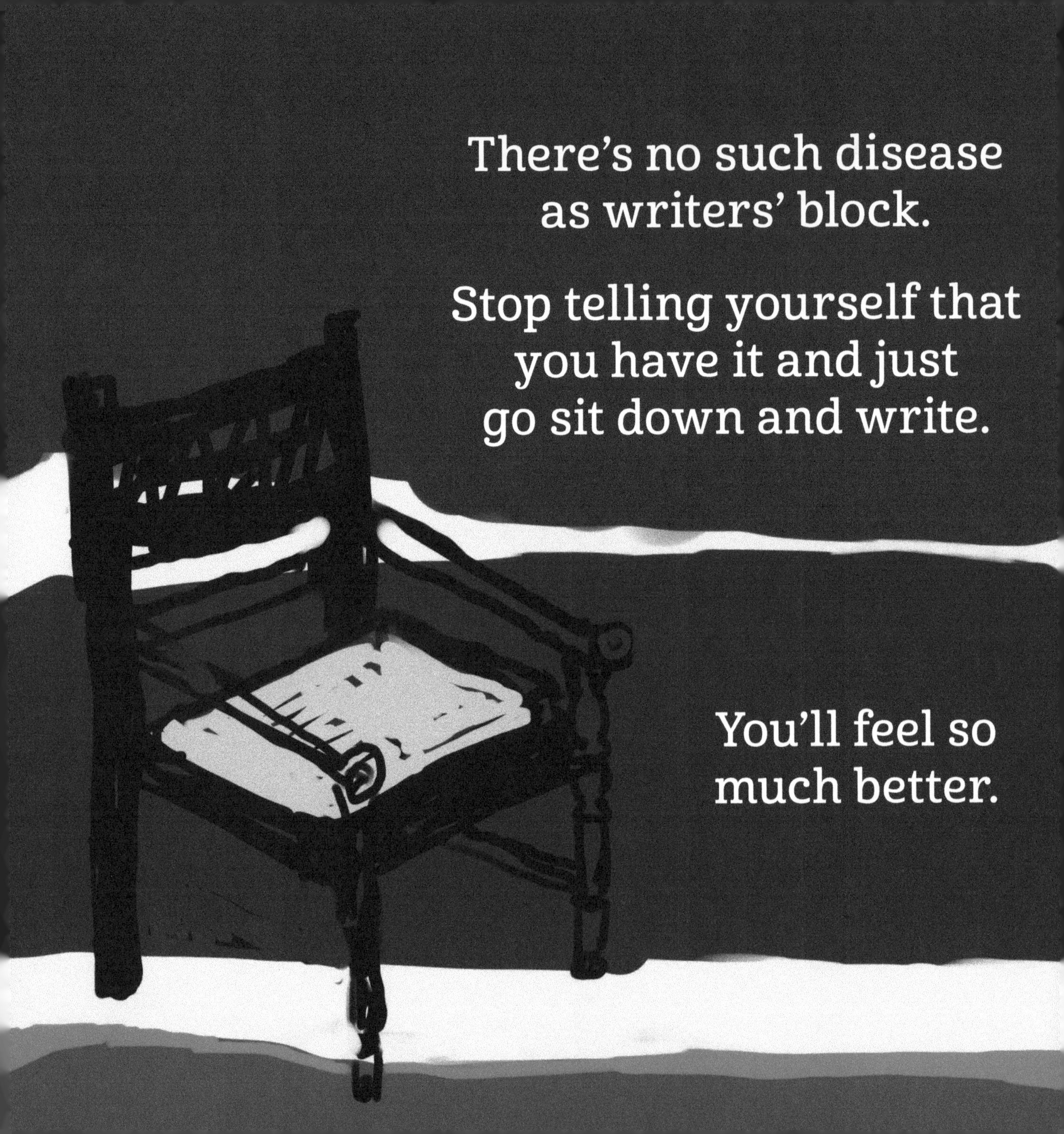
There's no such disease
as writers' block.
Stop telling yourself that
you have it and just
go sit down and write.
You'll feel so
much better.

PART FIVE: THE NET

A trapeze artist has a net in case they fall. Knowing the net is there, a trapeze artist can be braver and feel a sense of safety when they know there is something to catch them.

The outside and inside support system you create for yourself can keep you from falling into the abyss of existential loneliness and unhealthy artistic despair.

Feeding Your Life Force

The *Oxford Dictionary*'s definition of life force is: "The force or influence that gives something its vitality or strength. The spirit or energy that animates living creatures; the soul."

Many people don't feel creative because they aren't filling themselves up with the things that build their life force energy, which is at the source of all creativity. They may assume that if they have all their basics needs met (water, food, shelter, safety, sleep) they should be good to go.

There are things you could never give yourself or ask for because you'd risk knowing or being told you're too much, too spoiled, too demanding, or too sensitive. These may be things you tell yourself you don't deserve to have, or they should be only given as a reward after hard work. Do you question the power of the things that keep you vital, and at your best? Giving yourself the life force tank fillers, those that you may not feel are essential, can make a huge difference in the quality of your life. The alternative is to deny yourself essentials that you need to keep your life force strong. Such denial creates that sluggish, flat feeling you get when you're just going through the motions and following your obligations and routines.

It takes an honest inquiry to get out of that general malaise that hovers around your mind for no good reason…but how do you get to that and how do you know? The quantity and quality will vary, depending on you, but to help you think beyond that bubble, here are some common life force tank fillers:

- Quality time with friends
- Family time
- Puttering around the house time
- Laughter
- Physical touch

- Time spent in nature
- Time spent in doing hobbies
- Sleep
- Exercise
- Sex
- Affection
- Appreciation
- Time spent doing nothing
- Time spent alone
- Browsing through art galleries or museums
- Creative pursuits
- Meditation
- Spiritual connection

All of this varies for everybody. Some people don't need puttering time around the house, but absolutely fall apart if they don't get enough exercise, sleep, or sex. Ask yourself what fills you up and how much of it you think you need, then set boundaries with others, speak your truths, claim your time, and ask for what you need.

Here's an example of what I've learned about me:

If I exercise (six days a week) I feel vital, balanced and calm.

If I get creative expression (five days a week) I feel confident, proud, fulfilled.

If I have quality time with friends (several times in a week), I can be generous, grounded and patient.

It's easy to get stuck when addressing things you feel you lack, so here are some prompts to let you discover what activities tend to fill up your life force—and make you feel abundant. You may be surprised at the ways simple activities generate your state of mind and lift your energy:

- When I get at least _____ hours of sleep, I feel ________________________________ .
- When I get _____ minutes/hours of exercise in a day, I feel ______________________ .
- When I get _____minutes/hours of creative time in a day, I feel __________________ .

Make a daily commitment to give yourself what you may lack so that your cup can runneth over, you can be your best self, feel creative, and share it with others. You radiate with joy when you are filled up with life force. It shows in your energy, through your eyes and face and body movements. Your family and close friends appreciate the best qualities in you—just as you appreciate the best qualities in them.

When you keep your life force tank filled, you can be your best self and give back to others, so it's worth an investment. For instance, the people around you appreciate it when you are considerate, generous, patient, loving, sexy, or intuitive. How can you provide these qualities for others, yourself or your projects if you feel depleted? Can you be generous and selfish at the same time? Yes—of course you can—you're supposed to do this to live your best life!

Filling up your life force tank is a choice. Learn to give yourself what has been lacking so you can be your best self. Give yourself time for things that enliven you, like your art, so you can be generous and feel vital and fulfilled.

It's a win/win situation for you, and those around you.

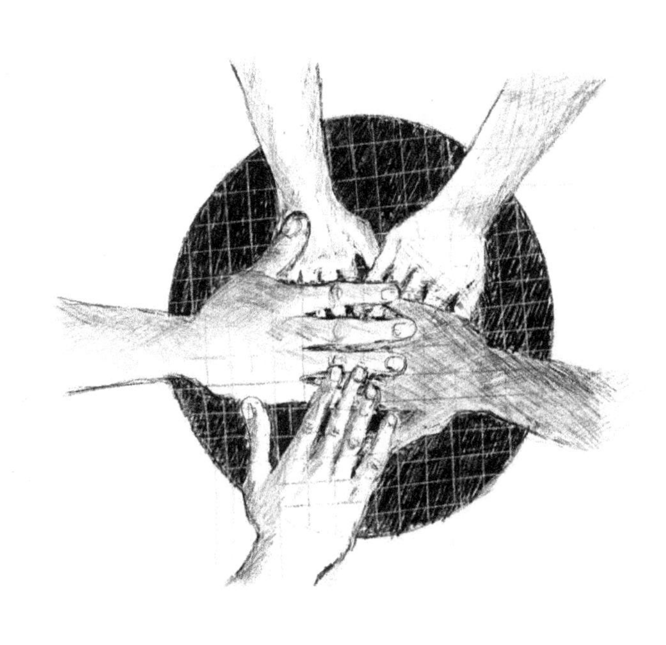

You Are Deserving

Most art making is solitary, but…you can't always be a hermit in a cave. You live with people. You might be living with a partner, raising children. You may have a job or volunteer work. In some way, you have responsibilities to others.

You may have a yearning—a need—to create, but you might feel like it is too frivolous. You may feel that creativity is something you can squeeze into your life, only if all the chores are done and you are alone. If you add five years more of turning your back on your longing, you will have given yourself (and locked in) the message that you do not deserve to get your needs met. You may feel that because your creativity time does not provide for others or make money it is not worthy of pursuing. When you turn your back on the expressions of your soul, you reinforce a materialistic and co-dependent society.

What do you teach your children if you continue to turn your backs on your deeper longings? You show them that obligation is primary; that life is meant to be linear and pursuing the curiosities of longing is not a worthy use of time or life. They'll see that soul longing can only come when all the work is done. They'll learn they should serve others at the cost of not serving themselves.

This type of thinking is a major cost and burden for the children you raise and to yourself as well. When you teach your spouse or partner that they are first and you are not as important, it is co-dependency in action.

Common reactions to the idea of asking for what you need in terms of distraction-free time and resources may sound like this:

"I feel like it's selfish for me to ask for time to write."

"It's not reasonable for me to paint when he's working so hard for the family."

"I feel like an entitled baby to ask for it."

"I should spend time with her on the weekends instead of working on my screenplay."

But you must know that your relationship to your needs when asking for creative space or time when you are in a partnership and/or parenting children is something to be questioned.

Is it true that your need for an hour in the morning or three hours in the weekend is selfish? Do you deserve to make yourself happy? Who are you when you give yourself the right to create? How do you show up in your family after you have had time to yourself with your art? Are you more patient? More sexual? More playful? Do you have the capacity to be more present?

Art feeds you. It is a nourishment that you crave but often feel like you don't deserve. When you have drunk from that well of creativity, you are more radiant, more present, more alive.

> *When I was a full-time parent for my two kids, and on the days that I would paint until it was time to make dinner, they would often come home and say, "I can tell you painted today, Mom." They saw it in my face. I was more myself. I was more alive. I was more present and patient with them. They would notice my clear energy, and generous spirit because I was not resentful that my creative energy had been spent doing the damn laundry!*

The capacity you develop when using the creative outlet and expressing yourself is profound.

> *When I am at my best, I can be funny, inspirational, empowering, radiant, and feel free. When I have been in the creative flow, I know that my tanks are filled, and I can more easily be the best person I know I can be. If I give myself an hour to paint, write or doodle, it provides me a sense of calm, peace, happiness, fulfillment that lasts about two days. Then, after a day or so I start to feel the something, which if ignored, will turn into anxiety. The people around me benefit from me expressing my creativity as well. I'm more patient and generous. I'm more*

playful and spontaneous. I'm feeling sexy and energetic. I'm more likely to say 'yes' to things because I have the capacity for them. I lose capacity for those wonderful qualities when I don't give myself time and space for my creativity.

Notice what qualities show up for you when you have done your art. Notice how long those qualities last in your tank before you begin to feel bereft and feel the call to express again. Notice what messages your body gives you when you have a need to create. You may feel:

- Anxiety
- Itchiness
- Bitchiness
- Cranky
- A lack of peace
- Edginess
- An ache in your solar plexus
- A tightness in your throat
- Exhaustion
- Judgmental
- Self-critical

These body or mood messages may be your soul calling you to your art.

You can
be selfish
AND
generous
at the same time.
Fill yourself up...
so you can be
generous to
others.

Paving the Way with Your Peeps

You have decided to commit to your creative project, your *one thing*, and you feel worthy enough to finally give it to yourself. In order to create anything, however, you need space and time. There's just one problem: you are not a hermit, living in a cave. There are those other people you live with who often get in the way!

How do you deal with other people who might get in your way?

The people in your life, especially if they don't identify as a creative or are not engaged in a creative endeavor such as you are, may not understand. Your creative time may disrupt the established norms in your household. Do you hold yourself back from asking for what you need for fear they may feel threatened from the time you take away from them?

The excuse model you may be tempted to use is to blame these other people for not pursuing your goals and dreams. Then you can tap into judgement and resentment and aim it directly at the very people you love. It's a lose/lose proposition. You are not doing the calling of your soul and are pushing the people you love away at the same time.

Everyone wants a happy mother/father/wife/husband/roommate. Giving yourself what you need to meet your needs is often inspiring to others. Setting boundaries without guilt or blame is empowering. Others will observe how your sense of your own worth grows and will be inspired by you. It may give them the right to do the same for themselves, with you as a model.

When Ed started working with clay projects in the living room after dinner, his kids started to work on their own creative pursuits as well. His wife, Sara, realized she could work during this time, and not just when the kids were at school. She illustrated children's books while everyone was working. They all stopped watching so much TV and felt like creativity had become a family affair. Everyone won.

Determining Your Needs

If you feel you deserve to create a life that fulfills you by making art, then communicating your desire lovingly and clearly to the people in your life is an essential ninja skillset. Before you do, it's important to get clear on the parameters of what you want to ask for, and to ensure that this conversation will not devolve into a bitch/whine/complaint fest. Complaints never work to bring about positive change as we all know, but we all forget sometimes. It's so easy to point your finger at someone else for why you can't get to your work. Because this is important to you and you need the support of the other, it is helpful to establish a time to talk. This signals your respect for the other as well as the importance of the topic to you. Significant subjects are treated with more care by all parties if they are scheduled, rather than casually tossed around when making sandwiches. Before you have the conversation with your loved one, get clear in your own mind about what you would need and prepare the way with them.

1. **Determine a reasonable space and time container that you need.**

   "I need one hour in the morning without interruptions to work on my book."

   "I need three hours every Sunday to sculpt my clay."

   "I need to go in the garage every night after dinner for one hour to paint."

2. **Take your complaint and turn it into a request.**

   COMPLAINT: My husband wants me to focus on him when I'm home and I never have time to play my guitar.

   REQUEST: "I would like to have two hours every Sunday without interruption to practice my instrument."

   COMPLAINT: My kids interrupt me when I'm writing, and I can never get anything done.

REQUEST: "I would like to be free to write in the morning/evenings for an hour every day."

COMPLAINT: Nobody ever respects my space. Everybody always needs me.

REQUEST: "When my door is closed, I'd like to not be interrupted."

3. **Make an appointment to talk.** When asking for a time to talk, say: "Could we set up a time to talk about______?" (Examples: Finding time when I can write. How to make some room in the garage so I can sculpt. Us carving out some time in our schedules so I can paint.) Then give an estimation: "I think it will take ______minutes/hours to discuss this with you."

The Request for Support

When asking for space/time/privacy to create, you may need a little support with the language you use. I believe these eight steps work well for asking anyone for the support you need in order to create.

1. Express appreciation.

When talk time comes, always begin with expressing gratitude for the things you appreciate. Appreciation always paves the way for a good request, or any good conversation. Make sure to show appreciation often with the people you love.

2. Enroll them into your dream.

People you love generally want to support you in the things that make you happy. They are not mind readers though, and don't often know what your deep longings or important dreams are unless you tell them. Using the language of your heart and deep-seated longings will help them get on board.

"I have realized that I'm feeling deprived of doing my art and I need some help."
"I would love to finish my book this year, but I need some support to do it."
"I know I would be happier in my life if I could find a time to sculpt."
"I have a dream to write and I could use some help."

3. Make the request.

"I need____________" (time, quiet, a space to work free of distractions).
"I need to write in the mornings/evenings for an hour every day."
"When I'm in front of the easel I need uninterrupted time."
"I would like to have no interruptions for two hours every Sunday."

4. Describe what having that support would bring to you.

"It would give me____________."

Speak in terms of how the support would give you a certain quality, energy, or feeling.

"If I got this time/space/support it would provide me with a sense of accomplishment."

"I would feel like I'm following my interests and dreams."

"I would feel happy and I would be more patient and generous."

"I would have time to finish my book and have time to focus."

"I would have the energy to play with the kids and be happy about making dinner."

"I would enjoy time with you afterwards and we could make dinner together."

"I would feel relaxed and peaceful."

"I would feel like having sex more because I would feel supported."

5. Describe your possible solutions.

"How it could work might be...________________."

"At lunch I will close my door and write."

"I will put a note on my door that says, 'Do Not Disturb' or 'Artist at Work.'"

"I would get up every morning an hour early."

"I would be at the computer for one hour every night after dinner."

"I will stay in my room at the desk and there would be no interruptions for a two hour stretch."

"I would go into the garage for an hour after dinner."

"I'll set up my paints on the porch and have quiet time there every Sunday from 3 to 5 pm."

"I will turn off my phone and not be disturbed so I can focus."

6. Ask for their ideas.

"Do you have any ideas that I haven't thought of?

"Maybe instead of the garage you could use the extra bedroom."

"What if we turn that potting shed into your art space?"

"I think you'll need some extra lighting."

7. Find the win/wins.

This is where you both look for the win/win or quid pro quo. You may get a considered response from your partner that sounds like a healthy bargain. This is about finding ways for everyone to get what they need.

"If I take the kids on Saturday morning and gave you space, would you take them on Sunday afternoon so I could watch the game?"

"If you do the morning shift so I can write, I'll put the kids to bed so you can work in the garage."

"You would get the kids ready for school, but then I would do the bedtime stories."

8. Follow up with appreciation for what is working.

You want to appreciate their efforts, whether it turned out perfect or not. Don't criticize or make corrections. Focus on the difference that time/space meant for you.

"Thank you so much for giving me that uninterrupted time. I got two chapters done today, thanks to you."

"I could have never finally started this book without your support."

"I feel so much more peaceful after I paint. Thank you for supporting me doing what lights me up."

I can guarantee the results won't always look perfect. Your kids will interrupt and ask if they can play with the clay or paints, too. Your wife will bring you the phone that has been ringing off the hook anyway. If you are consistent, however, the people will learn to acclimate and adjust to the new paradigm. If you set your boundaries clearly and steadily, you will notice that the kids may start to have creative time on their own or that your husband enjoys time with his own pursuits. What often occurs is everybody ends up getting more of what they want, not less.

I adapted this script on how to ask for support using ideas from Alison Armstrong, and information she teaches in her The Queen's Code book and "Understanding Men" online course. She shows that kindness is caring enough to tell the truth and ask for what you need. What if they could handle it and it brought you closer? What if asking for what you need would give them permission to step out of the routines and do something that lights them up as well? What if you were a role model for others to be their best selves?

Essie and her husband worked out a schedule so she could write in the mornings. He wanted more intimate time with her, but she often felt resentful that he didn't understand that she needed to write. After she used this script, he would do the morning routine with the kids and she did the evening. They ended up having more sex and felt closer. She expressed appreciation for him often and he was satisfied with their new arrangement and proud of her. She recently published her book.

Don't Gossip About Yourself

The outside world, particularly those not involved in their own creative pursuits, may not understand that the creative road is messy and comes with twists and turns and bumps. Their inquiries will only make the creator in you annoyed, especially when things are not going smoothly. Their responses will often be highly un-helpful and could further frustrate and discourage you.

They might ask you how your book is going when you are in a particularly rocky part of the journey. If you tell the truth to non-active creatives, "I'm really struggling right now," their response may not be helpful. "Maybe you don't really want to write," or," Well, you're not really a painter; you don't have any experience." Your Impeccable Artist will use this as an opportunity to pop up, rejoice and join them. And then you are even more wretched than you were before.

I often have the experience of needing to conjure up some of my Guards at the Gate when I get these inquiries or responses from "helpful" friends. You don't want to trigger their "helper" (who will not help you) into comments that might derail you if it hits you at a vulnerable moment.

Here are a few responses I find to be the most protective and empowering when people ask how your project is going:

"I'm right where I'm supposed to be." I like this because you are not judging the messy process of creativity. You are not putting yourself, your project or your muses in the position of being gossiped about.

"I'm learning a lot." Nobody can argue with this. Learning is a socially acceptable activity. And, you certainly are not telling fibs. Not only are you learning through the mechanics of your project, you are probably learning plenty about yourself. Maybe more than you ever bargained for!

In a nutshell, simply refuse to let yourself be gossiped about or gossip about your process. It's your business. Art is an individual journey. Nobody will understand unless they are on their own creative path.

The Creative Tribe:
We Who Believe
Each Other Into Being.

Find Your Tribe

If you have surrendered to the process of an artistic vision and a have willingness to carry through with that vision, you share something with fellow creative folks. You too have been vulnerable and courageous enough to make something that was not there before. You share traits to create an imagined outcome in the field of pure potentiality. You share using your imagination to make a new image in your mind from an imagined state. You share facing the voices of the Obstruction Army and know that every artist goes through some version of the same. So, when you hear another artist share their vulnerabilities and their self-doubts about their abilities, all artists will empathize. Together, you can share a companionable laugh. There is kinship between you like there is with veterans and astronauts.

I used to be surprised by it, but now I expect it. As an introvert, an empath, and someone who has been identified as "too much;" too sensitive, too dramatic, too excitable, (the list is long) early on in my creative life, I dreaded going into new environments to take an art or writing class. If the need and compulsion in me to discover and to learn new skills was great enough, however, I had to face the unknown of meeting new people. What I would come to learn is that artists are the most kind and supportive people in the world. Now, I believe I know why.

Artists are generous with each other. They share resources and tricks of the trade. I've noticed a profound lack of competitiveness amongst artists. Instead of hoarding their secrets that they have learned over time, artists know that creativity is limitless, so they are at the ready to help someone else. I notice that if a style is borrowed or copied, the artist sees it as a form of flattery, knowing it will morph into the others' personal and unique style eventually.

There is an abundance of generosity coming from these artistic souls in the world. While our society at large is based on competition and ambition to succeed, seasoned artists gave up that paradigm long ago. The paradigm of win at all costs, (I win, you lose) has nothing to do with the artist's journey or process. It is unreasonable to expect people who are not on an artistic journey to provide you with the quality of support you may need as an artist.

So much of creativity is done in silence and isolation, it is imperative to find your tribe of other artists. With too much seclusion or isolation, you can lose perspective, experience an imbalance of proportion, or develop an obsession with detail, combined with an inability to see the larger picture. Artists are a unique breed and when we find common souls who can support our work and efforts, it is a most beautiful and joyful connection.

Some great connections are one-on-one. To have someone else to bolster you when you feel like giving up, when you are lost, when you are on a tough learning curve, can literally make the difference in your work and your sense of wholeness and health as an artist.

Better yet, find a collection of people to form your tribe. There is so much power in a group of people with the same intentions. Do you know about Lynne McTaggart's book, *The Power of Eight: Harnessing the Miraculous Energies of a Small Group to Heal Others, Your Life, and the World*? It describes the collective power in mastermind groups, and meditation circles.

Every act of group cohesion starts with someone saying, "me too." The very best groups support each other to defeat daily the voices that want to keep everybody small. Therefore, it's important to have a tribe of fellow artists who can commiserate and cheer each other on for showing up each day. Group members can remind each other that anyone who has the courage to be raw and vulnerable and who can create, deserves a medal! Champion yourself, champion each other.

Take my writers group, for instance. I see us grow weekly. I see us supporting each other, telling the truth of the raw places, pushing the limits of what we have done before and encouraging the leap into new areas. People who are scaring themselves, like I am. People who have always been "too much," until they got broken open so they could be free. I feel so damn blessed to have them. We believe each other into being.

Go find an art partner, start an art salon, join a writing group. Share challenges. Have someone to share your work with, to not judge, but to celebrate that you both showed up to do some work. Any artistic personality knows the courage it takes to show up. You don't have to divorce your husband; you just need to fill your artistic social tanks with the life force essences of others!

So, go find your people. They are easy to see. You'll probably recognize a fellow artist by the twinkle in their eye. They look happier and bouncier somehow, more joyful, more playful. They don't quite fit the mold society tries to fit them into. If you notice, they will also believe in unseen forces and have a strong connection to their inner guidance system. This might make them trust themselves more and be able to tap into the field of unlimited possibilities. There is a glow coming off someone who had a good day making. Here are some other things you might notice:

- They can see the people who are like them, so they might recognize you
- They are more lit up
- They think outside the box
- They have a sense of humor
- They don't take themselves too seriously
- They are bored by convention
- They see their own restrictions and limitations and seek to move through them
- They are attuned to their body's messages
- Their common wounds have been the judgements of other people who were trying to put them in boxes they didn't belong in
- They are intelligent and know they learn differently
- They know that the more convention is embraced, the more restricted their bodies become
- They may be willfully naive and innocent

- They know that there is the part of themselves that needs to be protected from a world consisting of the resigned and the cynical
- They have a connection to something bigger than themselves

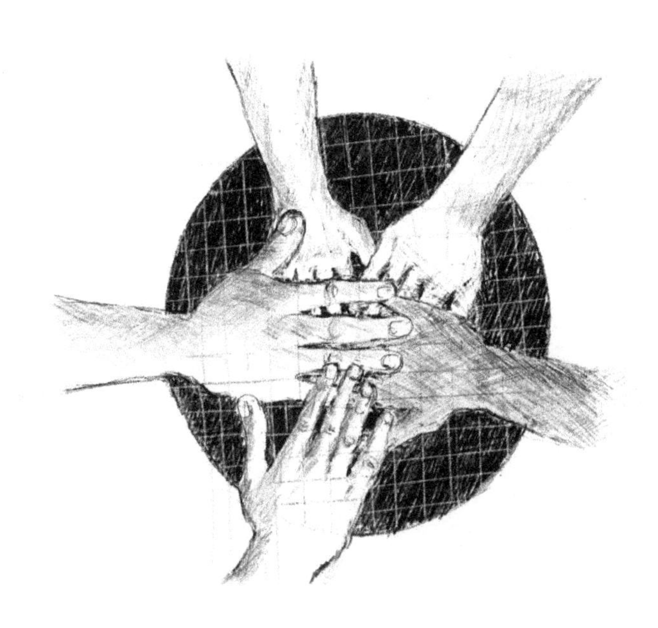

Don’t keep your
LIGHT hidden.
There are people
everywhere just
waiting for it.

Signs of Creative Awakening

As with meditation and spiritual enlightenment, the longer you spend in the alpha brain state, or *the zone*, the more you will be transformed. There is science for this, with the evidence of brain scans. In the alpha state your amygdala, the brain's fight-or-flight center, appears to shrink. As the amygdala shrinks, the prefrontal cortex (which is associated with higher order brain functions such as creativity, awareness, concentration and decision-making) becomes thicker.

As a result, your emotional reactivity goes down and your vibrational energy starts up-levelling. The more positive your energy is (high vibration), the more you will attract positive circumstances in your life. Also, the more you relate to your higher consciousness, the more room there is for you to receive messages from your guidance through signs and increased inspiration in your everyday life. A space is being created as a platform for the new possibilities to rush in.

You may feel unsteady as you learn to trust the process of transformation into being a creative. This book is meant to assist as you replace your sense of bewilderment with one of wonder. Here are some common changes I have witnessed in myself and my clients who experience subtle or dramatic shifts once they begin to creatively awaken.

- You seem to be attracting a different type of people
- You are developing a curiosity for new things
- You wake up with more energy
- You sleep better
- You have learned how to breathe and soften
- You are slowing down and becoming more present
- You have a feeling of deserving
- You are learning to set boundaries and can ask for what you want from the people you love
- Your relationships improve
- Some relationships fall away

- People you respect also seem to respect you and your commitment to your work
- People honor your boundaries
- You lose interest in gossip or drama
- You find yourself being curious about a variety of new things
- You can observe your thoughts and create more empowering ones to support yourself
- You are easily bored with ordinary things you used to do
- The urge to learn and discover more about yourself begins to outweigh the need to "fit in" with society
- You have let go of old beliefs about lack and find yourself appreciative of what you have
- You yearn for peace
- You see what beliefs need to be examined in exchange for inner peace
- You prefer quiet and peaceful environments
- You become more aware of subtle sensations in your body and your emotions
- Your ability to perceive expands
- You notice more about the world around you
- Your desire for freedom becomes stronger; following the crowd becomes unbearable
- You have an intuitive sense that something wonderful is waiting for you just outside of your comfort zone
- Your identity is expanding; you see yourself in broader terms.
- You laugh more
- You express yourself creatively in other areas of your life: cooking, gardening, dressing, decorating
- You're realizing your interconnectedness with people and things
- You are more appreciative of nature
- You lose interest in worrying
- You feel a confidence you have not experienced before
- Your priorities and values are shifting from the outward material world to the inner world of creativity

- You don't feel alone when you are solitary
- Your ability to pay attention and focus has increased
- You are less reactive
- Your memory increases
- You find yourself with a newfound ability to filter out distractions
- You find yourself more playful
- You don't take yourself too seriously
- You are kinder to yourself and others
- You are more willing to make new friends
- You have become allergic to superficiality and things/people that are not authentic
- Your five physical senses (sight, hearing, taste, touch, and smell) have become more developed
- Your spiritual senses have increased (intuition, emotions, imagination, conscience and inspiration)
- You have the feeling that something has changed inside of you
- You are less judgmental of others and see the goodness in them and yourself
- You are noticing color and have become highly sensitive to sound and music
- You have the feeling that someone/something is looking out for you
- You feel connected to spiritual realms
- You feel called to realize your dreams and your mission on Earth
- You are listening and trusting your intuition more and more
- You feel your feelings more, without identifying with them
- You feel sexier, more attuned to your own aliveness
- You notice an increase in "coincidences" and in "synchronicities" in your life
- Your inner peace has become of primary importance
- You are receiving images, ideas, music, and other creative inspirations at an surprising rate

- You have a new relationship to time; you often lose track of time when you are creating
- You believe your emotions are often a "compass" to guide you
- You are increasing your allowance for the energies of joy, inspiration, kindness, acceptance, peace, flow, passion, trust
- You have a sense of appreciation for who you are
- You feel that life takes another meaning when you create, you feel alive
- You lose interest in being and doing what others expect from you
- You feel sadness and compassion about the suffering in the world
- You are interested in how you can make this world a better place
- You have a deep yearning for meaning in your life
- You are developing a strong connection to animals and nature
- You have increasingly experienced the feeling of bliss
- You are often happy for no damn reason

A MIND
once
STRETCHED
into
POSSIBILITY
does not
return to its
original state.

AFTERWORD

I would like to share with you my own creative struggles in writing this book. I never wanted to be a writer. I thought, "Other people can sit around lonely and sweaty in their pajamas every day, but not me. I'm creative in other ways." Except there were ideas that kept poking at me to distraction. I wanted/needed/just had to share my ideas with others about creativity.

As they say, the pain pushes until the vision pulls. When it finally registered that these ideas wouldn't leave me alone (they were causing undue anxiety!) unless I wrote them down, I surrendered. I told myself, "Well, I can do it, I'm creative. It should be easy."

I was mightily humbled.

While I may have coached many people through their creative projects, including the writing of their books, (oh, I knew the right things to do and had gone through the process hand-in-hand with my clients) but, that could not and did not prepare me for the experience I was about to embark on.

I had never written a book myself.

I became my own lab rat for this book and the laboratory was harsh. It seems that when you ask for something, everything that's in the way of it is going to come up to be healed. I had entirely too many ideas and got overwhelmed. My thoughts were in a jumble. I knew my guides had abandoned me, my ego, my fears went on hyper alert, and every self-doubt in the world came up for me to question and try to slay. I lost focus, lost dedication, lost faith. My Impeccable Artist and I had a continuous brawl. She toyed and tortured me with her very bad, no good voices.

Feeling inept and irritable, I wanted to give up. I texted a fellow writer friend and said, "I must've been on crack to have said I wanted to write a book." But I couldn't give up. I'd told too many people about my stupid plans…what would they think of me being a quitter?

I also knew that I had made a promise to myself. And I know that once you make a concrete declaration to yourself and establish a resolve to act on it—well, once you decide—it's too painful to go back.

When I finally followed my own advice to create a dedicated chamber time, I made some progress. I slowly built up my capacity to withstand the intense vibration of *the zone* state, beginning writing from only 30 minutes a day to finally four to six hours, with lots of breaks. Some coherence in my head and heart developed, and the rhythms of my day settled in. I found myself in a nice little groove and became a staunch advocate for myself and my project. I became a radical believer in my own inner think tank, refusing to allow others to give me their bad advice and derail me. I got mad and started smack talking those very bad no good voices like a toughened street chick. Those voices began to quiet down and settle in the back seat. I kicked my social media addiction on its ass and turned off my phone. I began to think in terms of "garbage in, garbage out." I wanted to be cleaned up and cleaned out.

I began to trust my guidance and developed a new relationship to my muses. I began each day by claiming my writing time, relishing my progress at the end of each day. I found a tribe of other writers and authors who steadied me with their support. I found camaraderie with fellow brave souls who were doing the hard work of claiming their dreams despite pressure from the outside.

It has been an empowering experience to see possibilities beyond this project. It has bled into my life in ways I could never have imagined. I'm painting on another level, am braver about putting myself out there, I'm happier and feel a confidence I have never felt before. It seems the world opens for you when you let your light shine.

I feel like a light has been restored to me—one I didn't even know I was missing—all from a tiny seed of an idea that I learned to tend with a patience for each minuscule step. Something had been trying to find me and because I listened, finally, I was rewarded in mysterious ways. One of the rewards has been a frisky playfulness and an active relationship with the unknown.

I connected with a warrior energy at some point—something inside, something I've been calling, "That Which Pulls You Through." I don't know what it is, but it showed up one day; maybe it's the energy that grows fingernails or the force that can push that baby out of the womb, or the higher self, or God, or soul, I don't know or care. All I know is that writing this little book caused me to connect with my own "That Which Pulls You Through," and I am changed (in good ways) as a result.

I'm now left with a visceral understanding that there are no limits to creativity or spirituality. There is no limit to your capacity—or mine—to evolve and expand. Creativity is like the human heart; it's got room to go many places and it's got room for infinite expressions. It's as if I gave my heart back to itself.

My mother, Diane Coggins (an 87-year-old seeker and maker herself), said it best in a poem she wrote:

Return to Innocence

When the world feels
cold and stark
you've lost your way
back to your heart.
That place where
as a babe,
you could
just simply Be.
Practice the art,
and breathe through the heart.

Return you
to the you
you used
to be.
Let her splash. Let her sing,
innocence and freedom
she will bring.
Give her paint. Give her toys.
She returns your care
with unimaginable joys.

~ Diane Coggins, 2020

It makes sense to me now how when my clients begin creating again, they feel returned to their original selves. They make monumental shifts in their lives. You enter the creative field, unsure and often alone, and it has its way with you as your teacher. The act of originality has broad ramifications, and they are all encompassing; its tendrils reach into the body, heart, and spirit of a person. Creativity can heal wounds psychological and physical. It connects you to a guidance beyond your literal understanding. The rains and fires of creativity cannot help but teach you that by removing the brakes from your interior world, your exterior view can be liquid and yet burn with possibility.

Here's to the new possible; the curious and never-ending adventure of discovery.

It has been my humble pleasure and reward to be in service to your own creative awakening. When I think of yours, I cannot help but smile.

Kristina Coggins

When you take a
stand for yourself
and make art
every day, you
change your life.

When you put
your art out into
the world, you
change other
peoples' lives.